THE RIGHT OF
REVOLUTION

THE RIGHT OF
REVOLUTION
by Truman Nelson

BEACON PRESS : BOSTON

BY TRUMAN NELSON
The Sin of the Prophet
The Passion by the Brook
The Surveyor
Documents of Upheaval
The Torture of Mothers

TO ANNIE, WITH LOVE

THE RIGHT OF
REVOLUTION

I.

THE SOULS OF WHITE FOLKS

If you are for me and my problem — when I say me, I mean *us*, our people — then you have to be willing to do as old John Brown did.
— MALCOLM X, *Malcolm X Speaks*

If you can't see yourself as being in the context of John Brown, then bring me the guns.
— H. RAP BROWN, *National Guardian, Nov. 4, 1967*

We do not need paternal white "Big Daddies" for our friends now. What we need are some fighting John Browns."
— ROBERT WILLIAMS, *Revolutionary Action Movement Manifesto*

Virginia did not tremble at an old gray-headed man at Harper's Ferry; they trembled at a John Brown in every man's conscience.
WENDELL PHILLIPS, *Brooklyn, New York, November 1, 1859*

THERE is an irrational tyranny in the land of the free. From our very beginning we have been carrying on a war of violence and suppression against the black people we brought here. We held over four million of them as slaves, really disarmed warriors suffering all the evils of war in an involuntary servitude, and forced them to endure violations of their lives, liberties, properties, and every other "inalienable" right we claimed for ourselves.

This war is still going on against them, carried on day by day by our special repressive forces organized as "law enforcement agencies," or "riot police," or "tactical patrol forces." We have so many of these in the black communities that when its citizens make contact with the State, with *us*, it is always under the watchful eyes, or the flailing clubs, of police. They occupy the black ghettos like white mercenaries in a country under colonial oppression.

When the black people petition peacefully for the redress of grievances, they go unheard: when they act to be heard, they are called lawless criminals. When they turn to white people of goodwill, their revolutionary aims are vulgarized and emasculated into a futile dependence on parliamentary devices which have been tried and proven ineffectual for a hundred years. Or their revolutionary edge is blunted or liquidated in appeals to the conscience of the white man, who never stops feeling that the blacks are inherently inferior, and should only be admitted into this society on conditions of good behavior, i.e., that they act exactly like him.

This tyranny is most irrational when it refuses to admit that there has always been a moral and legitimate resistance to it, a slow, torturous, and *true* black revolution which can only end when the present form of government is changed to give political power to those who have none, and the dominant power to blacks in all political divisions where they happen to be a majority of the population.

Anybody the least familiar with history knows that this never takes place without a struggle, and a bloody one. We never educate our underlings to be our equals; they have to learn this in the revolutionary process itself. We have managed to obliterate or destroy any usable truths that should be available to them from their open revolutionary thrusts of the past: their Nat Turners, Gabriels, and Sheilds Greens, but the black revolution is surfacing again, from its underground streams flowing through American centuries, and it will soon stand erect and recognizable, and teaching itself to take power by the revolutionary process.

Tragically, it has to be a minority revolution, as all revolutions seem to be in their early stages. Whether this revolution grows into the will of the majority is our problem, not theirs. Long ago, they realized that if enough of us would go along with them, they wouldn't need a rebellion. But they have never been able to get more than a handful of us on their side, and they are tired of wearing out generation after generation, lives of deprivation and starvation in the richest country that has ever existed. They cannot wait any longer for us to purge ourselves of our racism . . . or to get over our panic that we might "throw out the baby with the bath water." They know that what we have here now is unable to end racism, and it must be irretrievably corrupt or erroneous no matter how many pieties, pleasures, and patriotisms are built into it.

So they are almost ready to go it alone. Some of them are confident that they will succeed, if only through the use of terror. They see us as so fat and soft, so in love with the delicate balance of our mechanized goods and services and their appetite-serving functions that we will panic and collapse at the first onslaught from the poor man's arsenal of attack . . . the Molotov cocktails, the lye and acid bombs made out of light bulbs, the acts of easy sabotage, cutting wires of light and power, choking sewers, jamming bridges, clogging roads, all the quickly induced malfunctions which a minority can bring to bear on all of our urban centers, simultaneously.

Somehow we have let them come to this . . . in their desperation, which is no longer quiet. We have *forced* them to come to this. And they, in turn, are going to force us to make the decisions inherent in our own desperation. They are calling out the John Brown in us. They are asking us to look inwardly and find out if he is there. I want him to be there.

I am white, not poverty-stricken, freer than most because of a certain nimbleness of utterance, too old now to feel or regret the loss of all the promises of the American dream. But I am sick at heart of the paralysis that will not let me be my brother's keeper; of the years and the agonies that let me know, fully as much as the black people, that my life in this country and its ideology have been a lie: that the whole testament of libertarian ideas and promises I was told to live by and defend with my life has been a pious fraud. I look upon our gross corruption of the rights of man, the ground rules that are supposed to order my daily existence here and know that to accept this corruption is committing a sin against my own senses, against the light that is in me. If I accept, without daily rising anger, these present, past, and future disparities in the human condition, I realize I am committing the greatest of sins, that of hypocrisy, which blinds a man to his own failings, and gives him a false idea of his position and purpose in the world.

Then out of somewhere comes a raging imperative, telling us act, act against an oppressor. Our observations and sensations of the nature of the world around us speak to us of the need for change. We talk about it, suffer . . . Thoreau said the conscience bleeds in times like these . . . But nothing happens, the rage dulls and disappears. Wendell Phillips called conscience the common sense of the masses. And so the American people are confronted with horrible realities every day which should stir their common sense and make it bleed. But nothing happens. It is agonizing.

On our TV screens this very night of July 15, 1967, we see our black brothers slipping suddenly and spontaneously into revolutionary action. Fighting the oppressor; making a Lexington Green out of their squalid streets and fetid houses. They are fired on, and they are shooting back. Now, at last, after generations of forced submersion, we can see a black resistance movement is being carried out. I see stout black men being thrown to the ground, lying there on their bellies, and being searched for weapons by white men in the uniforms of the United States government, and I know in my heart that this is the proudest position the black man has yet taken in this country, that they feel no humiliation from it, that they have finally got the oppressor on the run, fearful of them. There was a time when we had half convinced the black man that if he stood and bowed his head, or knelt and prayed for the white man to soften his hard heart, he would have his freedom. Freedom perhaps, manhood no.

We told them, through their own leaders that they had to match our capacity to inflict suffering on them by their capacity to endure it. That they had to meet our guns, clubs, dogs, bombs, sadistic police, white mobs like packs of mad animals, corrupt judges, hanging judges, with love, with "soul" force. When we bombed their homes, threatened and spat upon their little children as they suffered to come unto us, when we dragged them off the roads and beat them to death with chains, we said, But you must still love us . . . you will soon wear us down with your holy capacity to suffer . . . and when you win our hearts and conscience, when we discover the turning point in the longevity of our will to beat you and degrade you, you will overcome.

We have been telling them this for two hundred years, and doing violence to them, simultaneously, and continuously, between, and because of, the pious platitudes and programs of self-abnegation we have thrust on them. And we wonder why they hate us. They know that we do not think of them as citizens and men or we would have told them long ago to resist, by force, the tyranny and dictatorship of the landlord, the boss, the cops, judges, draft boards, hucksters, politicians, governors, presidents, and all the rest of us who will not get off their backs. We say that we are the

birthright possessors of inalienable rights, we cannot give
them away if we want to. Resistance to despotism is obedience to God, we say . . . to ourselves. But to them we say,
God is love, so love and hope and suffer in nonviolence.

It is obvious why we said all this: the next step leaves
only the alternatives of giving them all we have . . . or
revolution. The walls are tumbling down — everything is
fluid — boundaries are overflowed. What was secret, searing
anger — that which seemed to us only sullenness, envy, stu-
pidity — has rushed out to shatter glass, the hard transpar-
ency between us and them through which they saw our lives.
First the sound of shattering glass between our property
and them. Then the flame of gasoline bombs. Then shots
from the roofs. This may be telling us that the first alternative is lost already.

We had a chance to act this alternative out, legally and
peacefully in 1954 when the Supreme Court said that racial
discrimination was unlawful. It was our last chance because
here was a moment when the decision was unanimous and
the country in a mood to accept it. But then our paralysis
took over and we discovered gratefully the weasel words the
high court had put in for us; that we didn't have to make the
black equal to us right away, but with all deliberate speed. So
that in the five years following this decision it was quite all
right that about seventy-four black children were integrated
into primary school, that, by this demonstration of the meaning of all deliberate speed, we knew that it would take nearly
eighty thousand years for the two million, five hundred
thousand black children concerned to receive what has always been one of their inalienable rights.

Whether school integration has accelerated or not is
now irrelevant. Why count? We whites know that school
integration, like every other form of entrance into our society, is locked into stasis. It will take time, we keep on saying to this generation of black citizens, knowing that we said

this to their parents, each one of which had two parents, and four grandparents and eight great-grandparents, and so on into the thousands and millions we have been telling that it will take time. Now they know, as we do, that the gradualism expressed legally as "all deliberate speed" is only another way a great crime can become perpetuated in practice.

Now they know, because we have effectively demonstrated it in this fraudulent "ordered desegregation," that there has never been an instance in the history of the world where an oppressed people have been educated for freedom by their taskmasters. If the legal gradualism and the legal deliberate speed of the last two hundred years has not changed the human condition of the American black man and woman — forget it. It's not going to happen that way.

2.

WILL YOU GO, BROTHER, WILL YOU GO?

WE have got to the final solution the blacks want . . . not death but revolution. We whites prefer death to revolution; we would rather be dead than red and we have tried to press this on them and they are *visibly* rejecting it now . . . instead of silently and tearfully as before . . . during all those years when they would not learn from us and were so unpardonably "lazy" and "disorganized" and prone to "let us fight their battles for them."

Our death wish, among other reasons, has developed in us an extraordinary skill for cutting from the continuity of our history all revolutionary occurrences . . . or distorting their meaning in such a way that any confronting of domestic tyranny here is always reordered as the acts of madmen or criminals.

Already we are talking of the guns of Newark as fired in criminality and anarchy. The Governor, who suppressed it with "fire power" and blood, says, "The line between the jungle and the law might as well be drawn here as well as any place in America." He is giving the white official's view of every black ghetto and its problems . . . *the Jungle vs the Law.* And cops beating back the growth and power, the new green shoots of expanding life, beating them back with guns and clubs.

To me, the black uprisings of the midsummer of 1967 were authentic rebellions; they have not been suppressed, they are still burning underground. I look on them, respect them, and listen to them as revelations . . . as the catharsis white America needs to develop that sense of shame that is revolutionary. I know the simplicity of this is going to infuriate those *rational* and *responsible* people (who are responsible for these revolutionary preconditions in the first place and have already *rationalized* the rebellions out of existence) and those who want us to be so objective about the course of human events that they put down every warm-blooded notion or physical striving to rehumanize any people or persons. Let them cast this book aside, if they have not done so before. I am not writing this for the likes of these.

I am speaking to the black lads who keep up their truths and their taunts with the point of a white Guardsman's bayonet at their breasts . . . for the sorrowful white boys who lost their Karma when they had to leave the struggle for black liberation to the black men themselves. For the tortured mothers of the black ghettos who know their sons must either fling themselves sacrificially on the altar of freedom now, or become petty thieves, addicts, bums, winos, wife-beaters, male prostitutes, cops, or Uncle Toms. For the poor who have none to help them and who are being forever sealed into the iron cage of deprivation, hunger, cold, and filth, and above all, hopelessness. And for the few grown-up white Americans, and all teen-agers who know they have a birthright of revolutionary morality . . . who would neither be victims nor executioners.

I tell you this is not simplicity, it is purity. It is the text of the puritan revolutionary whose role it is to purify all acquiescence to corruptions and usurpations. He overlooks or breaks all laws which support racism and special privilege and exceptionalism. He feels that to do otherwise is a loss of revolutionary virtue and needs to be rejected out of hand. He feels it urgently and concretely when he hears that police in Newark, New Jersey, confronted black John Smith, taxi driver, and

> caved in my ribs, busted a hernia, and put a hole in my head. After I got into the precinct six or seven other officers, along with the two that arrested me, kicked and stomped me on the ribs and back. Then they took me to a cell and put my head over a toilet bowl. While my head was over the toilet bowl I was struck on the back of the head with a revolver. I was also being cursed while they were beating me. An arresting officer in the cell block said, *"This baby is mine."*

Is there anything wrong with a rebellion coming out of this? Out of this tyranny against John Smith, driving a self-rented cab just at dusk, with his fares far short of his $16.50 cab rent. Smith had accelerated his prowl for fares when a police car swung in front of him, driven by officers John De Simon and Vito Pontrelli.

The policemen drove very slowly, almost at a walking pace, looking for drunks and brawls on the hot summer sidewalk. They would not pull over for John Smith even though he blew his horn and flicked his lights time after time; they were baiting him. After having to tailgate the cops for a quarter of a mile, he tried to pass them. They cut him off, arrested him; there was the physical struggle, curses flung on both sides, Smith was thrown into the squad car and taken to the Fourth Precinct police station.

Harris David, a lawyer working for the Newark Service Project, which is carried on under a grant of Federal funds, and certainly no extremist group, felt that he had an airtight case against the arresting officers of atrocious assault and battery, false imprisonment, assault with a deadly weapon, assault with intent to kill, false swearing, false reporting of a crime, abusive process, disorderly conduct, creating a disturbance, and conspiracy to commit these crimes.

These last charges are interesting; almost every arrest in the ghetto includes them. Suspects are roughly handled and pistol-whipped; they are always charged falsely with assault on the officers. In order to make this stick, the officers falsely swear. The arrests are made in a disorderly way in which the suspect is unnecessarily pummeled and manhandled in a sadistic way. These brutal arrests almost always take place on the street, in the midst of a passing crowd or adjacent to windows overlooking them. It naturally creates a general disturbance. Their roughness and violence are deliberately used as an object lesson and a demonstration of police power to hurt — with complete immunity. This technique had become such a common practice that it must be planned ahead by the police as a fixed process, and therein lies the relevancy of the last charge, "conspiracy to commit these crimes."

Almost any one of these actions, performed in the sight of other black people, is a monstrous insult as much as a warning. That is the function of police brutality, the common catalyst in all these affairs. This, as a function, has become now so privileged and expected that when John Smith's lawyer went to the court with these complaints, with his client with him, ready for an examination on the truth of them, and wearing a six-inch bandage around his rib cage, the judge dismissed them and said the arrest was properly handled.

The judge, a James Del Mauro, who seems to be another bastion of Italian power, then gave his reason for the dismissal, the fact that the crime charged had been committed: "In these times of stress, with all the havoc and destruction, a policeman killed, a fireman killed, more than twenty people killed and 15 million dollars of damage, I am not accepting a complaint against the police." This kind of arbitrary separation of cause and effect is one of the worst forms of our destructive myopia.

The judge felt that John Smith was extremely presump-

tuous in presenting this complaint to the court after inad-
vertently starting the insurrection by the rumor of his own
death . . . and then turning up alive: "It was this particular
man if I recall from reading the papers, that originally
caused the rioting, when he was arrested and rumor swept
the colored community that he had been killed. He has been
paroled, he is alive, and there is nothing wrong with him."

After Smith had been to the police station and the other
black cab drivers began to spread the news on their radio
transmitters that Smith had been terribly worked over and
was on his way to the station house, everyone in the ghetto
knew it was possible that he would die there. They know
their local station house is a meat grinder for them; that
when you come out of there after an arrest it could be on a
stretcher, and there is almost always a beaten head. They
have learned through bitter experience that the police feel
that there should be instant punishment for minor infractions involving sassiness or an attitude of resistance between
the arrest and trial so that if the charges are unprovable or
dropped, punitive action, their idea of justice, will still have
been done. When the Mayor was told the next day that
police brutality had been committed, he allowed that it was
very possible and then brushed it off with one of the many
grim non sequiturs prevalent in this situation, saying he was
"asking the F.B.I. to look into it."

The knowledge the black people have about what happens to their brothers in police stations caused them to mo-
bilize around the station by the hundreds. It has never
been done exactly in this way before and it betokens a sharp
rise in the black revolutionary consciousness. In Theodore
Parker's day, in the old, white revolution, mobs like this used
to gather around the courthouses and harry the judges.

The crowd . . . let's call it a mob, since Martin Luther
King has re-created the moral mob of the abolitionists . . .
began to throw rocks at the station and to demand that Smith

be shown to them so that they could see whether or not he had been badly treated. This was denied them and they continued to pelt the building and threw three Molotov cocktails. There is a clear lesson here: If you arrest a black man where there is a big ghetto, treat him fairly, preserve all the amenities the law will allow, and show him to his friends, on demand.

Some "civil rights leaders" finally convinced the mob to move off and they, held together by their doubts and anger, smashed a few "token" windows and despoiled a liquor store. The rumor kept running like a fire in bush through the ghetto that Smith had been badly beaten, and by nightfall the next day, it was believed that he had died from a brain hemorrhage. There is no credibility gap in this sort of rumor among the black people. It happens all the time. A year or so ago it was verified that a black man is killed in the prisons of Mississippi every day.

The next night Smith's black guardians had swelled to over a thousand. They went back to the station to demand his appearance. When this was not forthcoming, they put the station under siege. Every window in the station was broken. The policemen were trapped inside until finally, in a flying-wedge counterattack, with flailing clubs, they pushed the people back. The avenging mob then turned to attack the soft underbelly of our business civilization: glass and goods. They began to loot every white-owned store in sight.

Mr. Fred Liederman of the Bilt-Right Furniture store says they took $20,000 worth of merchandise from him, mostly television sets. Monroe Bierman of the Fit-Rite Dress Shop says he lost everything, $50,000 worth of goods. Walter Wilderotter of Wilderotter's department store says he lost $175,000 in inventory. Gilbert Blumberg, president of the Springfield Avenue Merchants Association, says fifty percent of his fellow businessmen will close up and move away.

Those looting had no consciousness of guilt. It was an easy gig. Lookouts were posted at the corners and forty or

fifty people would pull down the protective steel grating
with a jolly heave-ho. Then they would enter and help themselves to their "self-service shopping." A woman told a reporter, "These stores have been robbing these people for
years and Negro businessmen can hardly beg, borrow, or
steal their way into renting a place on that street." The
police, completely outnumbered, could only drive their im-
potent squad cars down the street, pathetically blowing their
sirens. The looters would stop to throw at them anything
they could lay their hands on. One patrol car had all its
windows broken out before it could pull away from the
crowd. Stores known to be owned by black people were
passed over. And of course, the looting was carried out by a
small minority of the people of the ghetto.

At this point Governor Richard Hughes declared the
city in open rebellion. He called the looting an "atrocity."
When he came there he got a worse shock; there was an un-
canny mood of exultation coming from the black people in
rebellion. He said it was like "laughing at a funeral." But it
wasn't until later that he made the funerals. Hughes is known
nationally as one of the foremost advocates of "civil rights."
He was absolutely shocked that the black people were doing
this to him, after he had let them have so many peaceful
demonstrations whenever they wanted them — although they
never got what they wanted from them. He thought the rebellion was "a gross injustice to a fine city and a fine mayor."
Yet Newark has the highest national percentage of substand-
ard housing, the most crime per one hundred thousand of
population, the heaviest per-capita tax, the highest rate of
venereal disease, of new cases of tuberculosis, and maternal
mortality — and an estimate of a black population as high as
sixty percent. The Governor and the Mayor are absolutely
blind to this. How can they be otherwise when an "atrocity"
is a store window smashed and some merchandise taken?
There are no tears left for the smashed humans.

Coming in with Governor Hughes was his executioner,

Colonel David B. Kelly, the white commander of the New Jersey state police. It was he who ordered the funerals. He had the public assurance from the Governor that the trouble was not a spontaneous uprising against unemployment, hunger, squalid housing, police beatings, baitings, and constant cries of "Get the niggers" but was clearly the work of a "vicious criminal element" who would receive swift and retributive justice. Before he left town, twenty-eight black people got it.

Also under Colonel Kelly's command were three thousand National Guardsmen. The Newark city officials thought Kelly was a fine figure of a liberator. "He was very tough, honest, vigorous, impressive . . ." one relieved Newark official remembered. "He said: 'We didn't come to play.' " At the point when Kelly took over his combined command, "control measures hardened drastically." Over the police radio one order said, "Police, use your weapons, that's what you have them for."

The state troopers then went into battle against the blacks, armed with .38-caliber pistols, .30-caliber carbines, and .30-caliber M-I rifles. They were riding in armored personnel carriers, which resemble tanks, but they have no cannon. They clanked into battle, against the housing projects.

Confronting the threatening buildings "the police, state troopers and the National Guard spattered hundreds of apartments in the ghetto with machine gun, rifle and pistol fire. Many buildings had all their windows shot out during a search for snipers . . . Mrs. Eloise Spellman was shot and killed Saturday night by police bullets that were sprayed into her apartment. Young Bruce Spellman and his ten younger brothers and sisters had stood in the apartment and watched their mother die . . . A bullet ripped her shoulder apart and tore a hole in her neck.

Reporters watching the guardsmen and the police carrying out these summary executions on people for being black, heard this madness on the police radio: "Newark Police . . . Hold your fire . . . State Police . . . Hold your fire . . . You're shooting at each other! National Guardsmen, you're shooting at buildings and sparks fly so we think there are snipers . . . Be sure of your targets"!

Other Guardsmen moved through the streets of business with bayonets fixed, driving the unruly blacks before them. But the black men turned and taunted the guards, as they had the police and the state troops. They seemed to have no fear, no consciousness of their enormous guilt. When the guard had arrived that morning, coming through the white Italian section, people cheered them from every corner shouting, "Kill the bastards" and "Shoot the niggers." One National Guard captain told the reporters, "If anybody throws things down on us, then it's shoot to kill. It's either them or us, and it ain't going to be us." Carmine Ventola, from this same Italian neighborhood, was in the Guard. He talked to a reporter, "fingering a Saint Christopher medal" as he spoke: "I shot one of them in the leg. I didn't shoot to kill but next time I will. If the city ever gives them what they want there'll be riots out here!"

The massive military confrontation of the apartment houses where there were suspected snipers, the machine guns, the converging and grouping of vehicles, the stream of bullets pouring from the army side of the battle line was so intense that young black mothers tried to approach National Guard officers to ask for an armistice, or a temporary cease-fire, so they could evacuate the women and children and the "civilians." The blacks had accepted it as war; that is what they believe the white community is doing to them, *warring* on them.

"We're just about trapped in here," said one woman at Hayes House. "We can't leave because of all those guns out there and there is no more food left in the neighborhood." "I

haven't been shopping since last Saturday," said a woman
who lives at Scudder House with her husband and six
children. "We ate the last of our food — some spaghetti —
last night."

The black people who were not looters, not rioters, not
physically involved in the turbulence, cowered in dark and
hungry houses before the wall of National Guard fire; they
had no money, no food, no electricity, no elevator service
. . . even the water was knocked out by the savagery of the
military assault teams. Some food was finally brought in and
distributed to the people in the projects but those in the
dilapidated privately and absentee owned slum houses didn't
get any. "We ain't got nothing and we can't get anything,"
said a woman on 17th Avenue. "We got to starve just because we don't live in the projects?"

The New York *Times* says the most violent anti-Negro
feelings come from the Italian neighborhoods, the closest supporters of the Mayor and the police. Not one white man was
arrested during the trouble: although people in these neighborhoods had stoned Negroes and stood in the streets with
rifles in their hands.

The arrests, and most of the murders, had to do with
the "looting." In line with the profound qualitative change
and hardening which took place as Colonel Kelly took over,
stealing became "looting." The young blacks were now shot
to death for running out of some wrecked appliance store
with a $14.95 radio. This was no longer a routine police
matter wherein an observed thief was to be apprehended,
tried, and sentenced in a manner judicially commensurate
with the gravity or triviality of his crime. He had to be killed
— shot on sight. When simple thievery becomes transformed
into "looting" in the white property owner's lexicon, it is a
capital offense. It is a crime against the state, flat treason.
Instant, summary punishment has to be meted out.

The man "looting" knows the merchant steals from him;

that is how merchants survive, prosper; he buys cheap and sells dear as a profession, and in the selling dear he has to commit gross misrepresentation and fraud. This is his form of looting and he gets rewards and not punishment. *Caveat emptor* is his motto and morality for himself, but for everyone else: Shoot the bastard on sight. The black people know this; they are not deluded by euphemisms like "markup" and "merchandising." They know this whole country is a store with everything in it for sale and the only way they can get anything as "cheap" as the merchant can, is to "loot." They learned it from their Bible, which is ours as well:

> And the children of Israel did according to the word of Moses; and they borrowed of the Egyptians jewels of silver, and jewels of gold, and raiment:
> And the LORD gave the people favor in the sight of the Egyptians, so that they lent unto them *such things as they required:* and they spoiled the Egyptians.

"Spoiling the gyppers" is an old revolutionary tradition. The slaves did it. And John Brown did it too, for them. But most white Americans haven't been able to sweat their own slavery to private property out of themselves, and looting turns them off like nothing else. Every libertarian pseudo-revolutionary draws back and waits for something to happen that looks good . . . something pure, virtuous, uplifting, and, above all, sacrificial. It never happens that way. Revolutions are not pretty. Crispus Attucks was not pretty . . . he was black, raucous, and sometimes drunken, but he was one of our great revolutionary heroes, one of our founding fathers. The Boston Massacre was a completely unwarranted onslaught beginning with foul words and excrement thrown at a comparatively inoffensive and well-behaved British soldier, but by the time Sam Adams, John Hancock, Joseph Warren, and the rest of the Boston Massacre orators got through talking about it, it changed the world. It was "looting" to take the Englishmen's tea and drop it into Boston harbor, but John Adams had no qualms about it. He said:

> This is the most magnificent Movement of all, there is a dignity, a Majesty, a Sublimity, in this last effort of the Patriots, that I greatly admire. The people should never rise, without doing something to be remembered, something notable and striking. This Destruction of the TEA is so bold, so daring, so firm, intrepid and inflexible, and it must have so important consequences, and so lasting, that I can't but consider it an Epoch in History.

But no such romanticisms are needed to relieve the black man from his consciousness of guilt. Had there been no looting whatsoever, the houses where suspected snipers were shot at would still have been made a shambles and those stores, carefully passed over by the looters because they belonged to black people, would have been systematically shot up and destroyed by the lawmen themselves. Dozens of them had their plate-glass windows smashed by National Guard gun butts. A wrecked record shop had this sign in its window: "State Police shot up this store." Obviously the most lawless element in Newark was the law itself.

Perhaps Newark was not the way to Lexington Green or the Boston Massacre, but events are moving forward with great acceleration. A day or so after this, the small, well-off New Jersey city of Plainfield erupted and an incident took place there completely within the classic mode of revolutionary development. There was a search for hidden arms in the Plainfield ghetto, and Kelly, the brave butcher of housing projects, was again in command.

> We thought that if we could show them we were fine, respectable law officers, they would understand. If there are guns here, we feel the people would be only too glad to turn them in to us. We come to restore to this community the faith in one's fellowman to understand the problems of each other.

With these noble sentiments still ringing in the air, Kelly launched a spearhead of armored personnel carriers into a mile-square area of ghetto homes. The carriers were mounted with .50-caliber machine guns, and carried Guardsmen armed with M.I. rifles, .45-caliber machine guns and every other assortment of modern warfare. A state official, running desperately, was barely able to intercept this attempt to restore brotherly love to the community and Kelly's men were forced to carry out their search with only handheld weapons. Searchers confronted with a closed door used their feet and their rifle butts to force their way through. Inside they tore everything apart. "I could hear them tearing things up next door," said Maurice Brown of 309 Plainfield Avenue. "It sounded like they were coming through the walls." In the West End a Mr. Bowie kept asking, "Why would they do this? They would not do this to a white man's home."

This brutal onslaught on the privacy, the dignity, and the bare existence of these people's homes, carried out by New Jersey's head policeman, was a most egregious lawbreaking. He had no warrants; he had no right under any legal condition to do this. The Governor says that his proclamation of a state of emergency covered the case legally. But since when has a state been able to supersede the Federal Constitution? The answer is always, and at will. Governor Hughes or any other white politician with an army at his call can abolish the Fourth Amendment and the right of the people to be secure in their persons, houses, papers, and effects against unreasonable searches and seizures. And every other amendment and guarantee. They do it in the sacred name of "necessity." They have their necessities . . . and we have ours.

The point is not what legal rights Hughes and his executioner violated. The point is that the black people know he will not be punished but will be acclaimed for these days of murder and tyranny. And I know, as a white man, that these crimes against another race will rest on the conscience of my people lighter than the dust in the balance. For there is a vast sensibility gap between us. We do not *feel* their wrongs and hurts; we only know them. I write this from no special vantage point, from nowhere on the inside. The facts were taken from the New York *Times*. It is all common knowledge available to white Americans from what they have regarded for generations as their most unimpeachable source. It used to be that you only read such things in the radical press. Not anymore. There is no longer any need to conceal our society's discontents and crimes. They now let us know everything that is bad about our government or our soldiers in Vietnam, or our business leaders and institutions. They are not afraid of us, anymore. We have what T. S. Eliot called "disassociation of sensibility"; a rare and mortal disease of white humanity.

Every day the fluidness of profound social change, of incitement and event comes upon us, vast and uncontainable. It rushes like a river of searing acid through the pages of the national press. It never ends. We whites seem to be absolutely blinded by it. We never stop to question what it means, or if it has no meaning for us. In our blindness we brush it aside, waiting for our experts to explain it away for us. Which they will, with methods so bankrupt and futile that it will actually give aid to the revolutionaries bringing the wrongs of this society to their flash point.

This separateness in communication is going for them, for the revolutionaries. The same facts confront both sides. One sees them as insignificant, sees them with impatience, and feels that the facts can easily be answered by more force and violence. The other side learns, grows, experiments, simmers and explodes. These facts allow the revolutionaries to perform the most essential rule of liberative warfare: to keep the oppressor off-balance and continually making false judgments and tactical errors, compounding the urge and the need for spontaneous resistance.

The black resistance, in the past damaged and held down by the sensibility gap between it and the whites, can use this gap now to great advantage. The whites do not know what they are doing. They do not know that these rebellions, however tragic, are also inexorable and will keep happening, regardless of what cruelties and suppressions the whites employ their mercenaries to wreak on the blacks. The whites are so far from understanding that they cannot see that they are sowing fields of dragon's teeth and that we are supplying, over and over again, the best justification for nobly daring to be free.

We read in the New York *Times* that Major General O'Hara, the Commander of the New York State National Guard, feels that if his force were called out in a riot situation, "they might use greater force and firepower than had been used in other riot-struck cities across the country." It seems that more and more massive military attempts will be made to contain the black liberation struggle, of what is really black society's primal discontent. This white general, without consulting, in the slightest way, the People whose servant he is supposed to be, said he might order the use of hand grenades, recoilless rifles, bazookas and other heavy weapons. He said he would not rule out the use of any weapon in a New York riot.

He says he would be acting in support of civilian authority to restore peace and order, "but we would not be acting under civilian instruction," because such decisions as to whether you subdue a sniper in an apartment house which is the home for a hundred families by massed machine gun fire, by hurling grenades into its windows, or by blasting down its walls with bazookas have to be made by him, and him alone, because "civilians are not cognizant of these matters." I'm sure the civilians in the house under siege will be quite cognizant of them and it will not be long until the single sniper is joined by every man and many of the women in the place, exerting their civilian rights not to be shot at and killed by their own mercenaries. It is obvious that O'Hara, like his associate Kelly in New Jersey, does not feel that the people in the ghetto are even civilians. "He said that to some extent the military methods used in flushing guerrillas out of a village in Vietnam could be adapted to guerrilla warfare in the ghettos." This is blindness that is nearly subhuman. I am sure that O'Hara does not feel himself to be a tyrant, or an operative unit in a system of tyranny. He could be a member of the NAACP.

A great qualitative change came to the American scene when we saw the civil-rights struggle unfolding and people slugged by the police for demanding what was newly guaranteed to them, or for merely getting to their knees and praying for it. The repression of the blacks was never that obvious before. Liberty was tolerable because we never really asked for it, or used it in that simple way. We did not seem to realize that after the interminable desegregation debate, brought to its moment of truth by the Supreme Court decision of 1954, the blacks were going to test it, and our sympathies and sincerities, by some sort of practical action, including direct violence. We were able by our dearly purchased sophism of "nonviolence" to stave off a real test for half a decade. But our time has run out on this and when some clear example of police brutality takes place the blacks are going to act against it by rescuing the arrested and accused before they are tortured in the precinct house, or failing this, they are going to storm the precinct house. Or they are going into direct, physical reprisals. They are going to fall back on that revolutionary morality which holds that all ordinary rules of the game are set aside once an oppressed people start their uprising . . . that anything goes, in war, or revolution. They are going to become "all transcendental," as Thoreau says John Brown was. Emerson said that once a man is driven to asserting "the sovereign rights which the majesty of his being confers on him . . . he would assassinate like Timoleon . . . resolve on suicide like Cato . . . commit sacrilege like David, yea, and pluck corn of the Sabbath for no other reason that I was suffering from lack of food."

There is no question, on reading the accounts of the police, state trooper, and National Guard invasions of Newark and the other ghettos, that an intrinsic state of war exists. Almost every observer has noted that the government forces go into battle shouting racist slogans: "Get the niggers" or "Die, you black bastards" was the indisputable battle cry. It is also indisputable that in this war the greatest acts of injustice and the most appalling sacrifice of human life are all on one side. Many liberals respond sympathetically to the weaker side and give vocal assurances of their understanding. They are already making plans to do something for the survivors. But what if the situation was reversed, and instead of two cops and thirty or forty blacks in each case, it was thirty cops and two blacks that fell dead in the bloody streets? Where would their sympathies be then?

Suppose the white liberals had it in their power to cause this reversal of statistics? Would they do it? For all their talk about the death-life of the ghettos and its putrescent evidences of racist oppression, it is very doubtful. But if they support the black side at all it should be in victory as well as defeat, for the moral circumstances which brought on the uprising are not changed by the result. If the black man is justified at all, he is justified in winning . . . in putting down his oppressor.

Our President, in explanation of the bombings just carried out at a point dangerously near the China border, justi-

fied them by saying, "we are going to do everything we can
to protect the men we have there." He being witness, should
not the white liberal who is irrevocably committed to the
fight against racism, and to full brotherhood with the black
man, have a duty to "protect the men we have there" — in
the ghetto — and to support the forces of black resistance to
that mass police invasion which brings about black massacres? Should not his voice be raised saying it is better to
battle to save the oppressed, and do what is just, than to have
the lives of the oppressed destroyed by the police in order
that injustice may be continued?

Our President being witness, should not every white
man who would fight with deadly weapons abroad to "protect his liberties" encourage and even incite the black men
under the policeman's club and the landlord's unlawful
gouging to resist both tyrannies, and help furnish them with
whatever means they need, or they chose to carry out this
purpose?

Most white liberals support insurrections of an oppressed people all over the world. And at the same time they
have no hesitation in telling the American black man how
oppressed *he* is. They flood his revolutionary consciousness
with testimonies, reports, analyses, dissections, proving there
is a tyranny against him in the jargon of every scholarly
discipline. What they are saying amounts in the end to this:
"You have a cause and a just one, but you must never think
of rebellion; it can't work, it can't win. You are doomed forever to a cause without a rebellion."

In spite of this, in a little more than a week's time,
rebellions took place in Newark, Plainfield, Hartford, Mont-
clair, Orange, Minneapolis, Nyack, and other points west
and south. There have been uprisings in New York, Chicago, Philadelphia, Detroit, San Francisco, Oakland, Boston,
St. Louis, Washington, Cleveland, and Baltimore — cities
that contain over thirty-one percent of the American black

people. Then there were the Buffalo, Rochester, New Haven, Fort Wayne, and San Diego upheavals.

The Attorney General of the United States and the FBI have found no evidence that any of these have come as a result of outside agitators, or have been formulated in advance, or in concert. They come gushing forth, as from a parched earth when the water table has been restored. The black people have been appealing for generations to the conscience and reason of the white Americans. In these recent years of rebellion they have learned the efficacy of appealing to our fears. Their insurrections have brought more bread into the ghetto than a century of prayers and tears. They are even winning elections because of them.

But all the parliamentary tokenism, all the sops of poverty programs, cultural compensations, all the tricks of the sociologist's trade are not going to turn the rising tide of the black resistance to anything less than full control over their own social and political destiny. We should say, as Garrison and the Abolitionists said, "success to every insurrection in every slave country." They are going, whether we want them to, or "advise" them to, or not. The only question before us is, will we go with them when the time comes; will we hail them, and justify them; will we save our mourning for those who fall under the policeman's bullets, rather than react, in fear and trembling, to the disrupting of our business civilization? The right and duty of the oppressed to go up against his oppressor is unquestionable.

3.

NO RIGHTS, NO DUTIES

THOMAS JEFFERSON, when queried about the authority, legal and otherwise, for his revolutionary assertion that people have a right to overthrow their government under certain conditions, said:

> All its authority rests then on the harmonizing sentiments of the day, whether expressed in conversation, in letters, printed essays, or the elementary books of public right, as Aristotle, Cicero, Locke, Sidney, etc. . . . it was intended to be an expression of the American Mind.

It was just as plainly understood by the founding fathers that all government is a contract, and if it gives no rights, or even diminished rights, you owe it no duties. What allegiance, really, can this government demand of a group commonly known as *second-class citizens?* The same is true of *paupers* and *minors.* They are never given the equal protection of the laws. The poor are confined by economic attrition in slums where violations of housing and health codes are carried on with impunity every day. They could not exist as slums, otherwise. The minors, healthy young boys under voting age, are forced into an involuntary servitude in the military establishment, which demands of them that they kill or be killed in countries far away for purposes which they consider irrelevant to the point of madness. As minors, they have no rights that a legislator needs to respect.

The American people as a whole, even the affluent, seem to have lost control over their own politics. They know that faceless men at the levers of power in the Pentagon can throw a switch to oblivion for the world without even considering asking for the consent of the governed. Many of us are finally getting this straight in our heads, but they have got to us lower down and made us political eunuchs. We are so squeezed by our "responsibility to the free world" that we cannot have a free thought but what we are warned that the whole "free world" will go down if we act on it.

Political emasculation is not our only organic change. The simple facts of the Newark rebellion reveal that the total organism of American life is rotting faster and faster into putrefaction. The stinking decay grows in our guts, and when we try to cure it, they break in our hands. One of our most sacred rights, that of the individual, *individualism,* forsooth, is now debased and swept away with the full connivance of the elected powers.

The crimes, if any, in Newark, were carried out by individuals. A few armed men, estimated by the police as not over ten men, with names, personalities, and motives of their own (men feeling perhaps, that they owed no more duty to this government than the Irish did to the British Government in the beginning of their revolution) fired at our police and our soldiers. A whole people was punished for this. Mortal punishment in a rain of fire went sweeping into the apartment houses and killing the innocent.

It is nowhere known for certain if any snipers were killed by the police, and it never will be known because the police have moved into simple warfare where the trajectory of function is to find the locus of the enemy and flush him out with firepower. And to act, with the greatest immediacy, not against a suspected individual, but against a flawed totality. Thus our nationalism has reached its apogee. No longer can a man stand and bargain with his government over the extent of his rights and duties, his innocence or guilt, as our forefathers did, even with their God.

This new point of view, the consciousness now formed which demands that we punish collectively for individual guilt, we are acting out all over the world. The most important task assigned to us as a nation, the leading and generating fact of our lives, is the war we are carrying on in Vietnam, a war against a total people, wherein it is a routine function to bomb and burn a whole village because it is suspected that one or two of the active enemy are located there, or have always lived there.

How can we think that in performing this, which even our apologists characterize as a cruel and *dirty* war, that our actions will not stain through our whole consciousness and benumb and degenerate us in our wholeness and make us act toward ourselves as we do toward others?

The fact is, what the rich man does to the poor man, what the landlord does to the tenant, what the merchant does to the consumer, what the boss does to the worker, what the policeman does to the suspect, what the jailor does to the helpless criminal in his power is only a local reflection of what we are doing as a nation abroad with our armies. And as the merchants, police, judges, landlords, bosses, jailors increase at home, while our soldiers escalate their presence abroad, so does the scope and intensity of their action against their victims.

And all the time we are told that to suffer this is part of the *duty* we must pay for our *rights*. That these acts which they say they perform only as a cruel necessity are saving us from being the victims of evil men, somewhere else, or evil systems, over there . . . who will only use us for their gratification. That if they let up for a moment their heavy-handed control of our lives, it will provide the vicious and unprincipled a chance to oppress the innocent. So, although some individuals may question some of the acts performed by those in power . . . they must continue to rule us for the greater good.

This means that they, our overlords, are all virtuous, all compassionate, all understanding public servants who took up the cross to suffer and sacrifice in carrying out their tasks and duties to us . . . that it is their duty to curtail our rights because they are carrying out a responsibility to law and order and the greatest good.

We, on the other hand, have to accept their acts of usurpation and control as our *duty* and promise on our oaths that we will unquestioningly obey their commands as spoken and enforced by their myriads of overseers, spies, interrogators, and whippers-in, from the President to the local draft board and social worker. And cheerfully recognize their rights to the lion's share of our daily labor so they can carry out their duty to control us with a maximum efficiency and have a gracious surrounding in which they can unwind, after a wearisome day of holding us in an appropriate system of checks and balances.

And we must carry out, proudly and cheerfully, our right to mark, every four years, a cross beside some names printed on a ballot . . . names of men either completely unknown to us, or only too well known as scoundrels, windbags, and embezzlers who have lived all their lives on the public payrolls and prospered well beyond the million mark. And although we know, from the experiences of ourselves, our fathers, and grandfathers, that regardless of the inane speeches they utter, promising change, they will do the same as the men in office before them and before them and before them, and they will plead the same crises of the Republic, plead the same urgencies and imperatives about the obscene Vietnam War of 1967 as they did about the obscene Mexican War of 1847, and in about the same words.

We must also perform the right and duty of serving voluntarily in the courts, and sitting in judgment on other frail humans; knowing that by the time the government prosecutor and the government judge get through with the case we will still not know much about the guilt or innocence of the accused or be able to do anything about it if we did. All we have to do is be the face of the rubber stamp which the clerk pounds on the face of the man on trial which says, The people find you guilty and sentence you to prison and torture for your life's duration.

And finally, we must always consider it part of our rights and duties that, no matter how decent, how politically and economically advanced, how humane, gentle, and loving we know people in other nations to be, and no matter if the cause they are fighting and dying for is to overthrow the yoke of centuries of exploitation and despotism, we must be prepared at a moment's notice to look on them as deadly enemies threatening the very foundations of our homes and be prepared to burn them, starve them, torture them, kill them, and do the same to all others who do not regard them as deadly enemies because of government fiat, even though these others may be our own sons, brothers, fathers, lovers, and friends. Laws, lawmakers, or law-enforcers who do this are not to be considered laws, nor lawmakers, nor law-enforcers, and should be resisted as any usurpation or usurper should be, at all times.

The self-evident American right of revolution lies in this: that an unconstitutional law is not a law. An unconstitutional law can be defined, in revolutionary terms, as one against the people en masse, and for special privilege. It should be just as opposable when it is against *a people,* living within the confines of the United States. It is thus clearly not agreed on by all the people.

An officer of the government is as any officer "of the law" only when he is proceeding according to law. When he is killing a woman in an apartment house that may or may not be the location of a sniper, he is not acting in a lawful way. The moment he ventures beyond the law he becomes like any other man. He forfeits the law's mantle of immunity and protection. He may then be resisted like any other trespasser. A law that is palpably against the peace and security of all the people, such as all the racist laws on the books of the Southern States, laws limiting the rights and privileges of privacy and movement of the blacks in the Northern states, the laws against the Indians in the Western States, and those against the poor in all the states, is really not a law at all, constitutionally, and is thus void and confers no authority on anyone, and whoever attempts to execute it, does so at his own peril.

Common sense, the conscience of the mass, will tell you if this doctrine is not valid; then anyone with police power can usurp authority, and sustained by these unconstitutional laws, can treat people as he pleases. Many have already done this, are doing this, and still we wonder why we can't get these usurpers off our backs. A self-proclaimed "law-making body" or "law-enforcing agency" can beat, rape, torture or kill at will — as such bodies do now, in Mississippi, and have for over a century — and the people have no right to resist them. It simply does not make sense. The best of our founding fathers wanted the law to make sense . . . wanted a "government and policy on such plain and obvious general principles, as would be intelligible to the plainest rustic. . . ."

The true revolutionary, then and now, holds that the Declaration and the Constitution contemplate no submission by the people to gross usurpation of civil rights by the government, or to the lawless violence of its officers. On the contrary, the Constitution provides that the right of the people to keep and bear arms shall not be infringed. This constitutional right to bear arms implies the right to use them, as much as the constitutional right to buy and keep food implies the right to eat it.

The Constitution also takes it for granted that, as the

people have the right, they will also have the sense to use arms, whenever the necessity of the case justifies it; this is the only remedy suggested by the Constitution, and is necessarily the only remedy that can exist when the government has become so corrupt that it can offer no peaceful solution to an intolerable way of life.

It is no answer to this argument on the right of revolution to say that if an unconstitutional act be passed, the mischief can be remedied by a repeal of it, and that this remedy can be brought about by a full discussion and the exercise of one's voting rights. The black men in the South discovered, generations ago, that if an unconstitutional and oppressive act is binding until invalidated by repeal, the government in the meantime will disarm them, plunge them into ignorance, suppress their freedom of assembly, stop them from casting a ballot and easily put it beyond their power to reform their government through the exercise of the rights of repeal.

A government can assume as much authority to disarm the people, to prevent them from voting, and to perpetuate rule by a clique as they have for any other unconstitutional act. So that if the first, and comparatively mild, unconstitutional and oppressive act cannot be resisted by force, then the last act necessary for the imposition of a total tyranny may not be.

The right of the government "to suppress insurrection" does not conflict with this right of the people to resist the execution of laws directed against their basic rights. An insurrection is a rising against the law, and not against usurpation. The actions, for example, of native fascist groups can be demonstrated by their own public acts and statements to be designed for privilege for themselves and to be defamatory and oppressive to other groups among the people. The black people don't want the police to shoot into white working-class apartments either.

The right of resistance to usurping laws is in its simplest

form a natural defense of the natural rights of people to protect themselves against thieves, tyrants, monomaniacs, and trespassers who attempt to set up their own personal, or group, authority against the people they are supposed to serve. It is the threat of the power of the people to remove them by force that keeps officeholders from perpetuating themselves. Not that they are any worse than other men, but the rewards are great and most of them act as though they were trying to discover the utmost limit of popular acquiescence to their self-exploitation and small tyrannies. In sum, if there is no right of revolution there is no other right our officials have to respect.

By no means am I saying that this is the prevailing concept of our organic law among the leaders and pundits of the country. Although they might, if pressed hard enough, give lip service to it. Arthur Schlesinger said in the *Atlantic Monthly* that the American concept of the right of revolution was the greatest idea we have given to the world:

> First and foremost stands the concept of the inherent and universal right of revolution . . . proclaimed in the Declaration of Independence: the doctrine that "all men are created equal . . . possessing inalienable rights to life, liberty and the pursuit of happiness" with the corollary that governments derive their just powers from the consent of the governed and that therefore the people have a right to supplant any government "destructive of these ends" with one they believe most likely to effect their safety and happiness. True, the history of England provided precedents to the men of 1776, and the Age of Enlightenment supplied intellectual support; but the flaming pronouncement, followed by its vindication on the battlefield, made the doctrine ever afterwards an irrepressible agency "in the course of human events." Europe was the first to respond . . . A series of revolts overturned, or strove to overturn, illiberal governments through most of the Continent, and hastened popular reforms in other lands to forestall popular upheavals. These

convulsions all had their internal causes but in every instance the leaders derived inspiration from America's
achievement of popular rule, as well as from its freely expressed interest in their similar aspirations.

"The Declaration of Independence is our Creed," Supreme Court Justice Douglas said, in an article on "The U.S.
and the Revolutionary Spirit." He said we should not be
afraid to talk revolution and to voice our approval of it. He
tells us to become the active protagonist of the independence
of all people. Go up against the darkness and pain of continuing feudalism. "There is a political feudalism where a dy-
nasty has the trappings of a parliamentary system but manipu-
lates it for the benefit of a ruling class . . . Revolution in
the twentieth century means rebellion against another kind
of feudalism . . . economic feudalism . . . the United States
should promote democratic revolutions against these conditions of economic feudalism."

Going back, we find John Locke's dictum, in his essay
on government, that when the natural rights of man are
violated, the people have the right and the duty of suppressing or changing the government. "The last recourse against
wrongful and unauthorized force is opposition to it."

It is the massiveness of the display of force against them
that has brought the black people to their revolutionary
flash point more than anything else. They know, as soon as
they hear the sounds of masses of police sirens that their little
insurrection, or their little rebellion, or their small act of
resistance will turn into a massacre, not of the enemy, but of
themselves. But yet they go on resisting until the local police
sirens are replaced by the clank of tanks, or personnel carriers; the clubs, the police revolvers are superseded by bayonets
and death-spitting machine guns. And still their exultation
grows, an exultation that is absolutely inexplicable to the
whites, seeing them surrounded by the massacre of their own
people. Sartre speaks of this; of how the Frenchmen of the

Resistance never felt freer than when they were under the attacks of the Nazi S. S. How the more they were condemned to silence, the more they felt that they were approaching liberation.

These rebellions by the blacks are a minority action: they cannot succeed militarily, and nobody thinks they will. The whole process is a *telling* revolution, a way of stating something buried under centuries of apathy and indifference far worse than omnipresent opposition. A *Life* magazine interview with a black sniper reveals this. He is not trying to kill cops and Guardsmen. When they are struck down it is by accident. He is trying, he says, to tell "our people we are here." And in the process, "the firing of five or six shots in the air is enough to draw cops thick as fleas on a dog and still give time to get away." Then the people take what they want.

But it is much more than that: the black insurrection-white massacre method of telling revolution is in some ways comparable to the Buddhists burning themselves to tell of their to-the-death commitment to their country's revolution.

I always felt that an enormous amount of time, money, and effort was wasted in the last years of the civil-rights crisis, while the leaders, black and white, were trying to convince the American black man that he was really a downtrodden Hindu, a palpitating mass of ingrained and inborn submission, a victim of a caste society which stretches back, almost to prehistory. The Hindu, or to be more specific, the followers of Gandhi, were victims in a land so impoverished and barren that a lifetime of starvation was, and is still is, their common lot . . . a land where living is so hard that men want a God so they can hate him as the father and ordainer of their degradation.

The American black man is a citizen in a rich land, with a citizen's rights and duty to resist, resist all attempts to deprive him of its manifold blessings. Even if he doesn't *want* to resist, he must; it is his duty, as it is the duty of all honest whites to urge him and support him in the process. Why should he have been urged to go through all this Hinduizing to regain the rights he already had in 1776? He was here then and fought alongside of the whites out of the same revolutionary morality, for the same revolutionary rights he is dying for right now . . . the idea that men before the law are exactly equal and that no man can take away these equalities except as forfeiture for a crime adjudged and confirmed by ancient and democratic due process.

Legally he has always had these rights. They were taken away from him by force and fraud. When the racist laws were written and enforced and then upheld finally by the Supreme Court of the United States, it was the lawbreaker and should have been resisted. The black man did resist these racist laws, but in vain. Police, militia, Federal troops beat him until he went down, over and over again, a victim of blood and violence, his land looted, his home burned, his daughter raped, his son lynched, his babies starved, his progeny for generations suffering automatically the same fate.

When he was finally handed the weapon of "soul force" he tried it; no one can deny that he honestly gave it a try. But we are living in a lunatic society, a racist society that will never stop hiring cops and soldiers to beat him until he stops them . . . or we stop the hiring. If we say the black man is a citizen, then he has a clear duty to resist tyranny and dictatorship, legally and peacefully if he can, forcibly if he must. He is the birthright possessor of the same rights we have. He cannot give them up if he wants to. He was not born to be a victim to test the longevity of our desire to oppress him.

Take a good look at the *Life* magazine for July 28, 1967. Look at it before it lies dog-eared in the dentist's office, or slides to oblivion in the trash trucks. Before the eyes of one of its reporters and cameramen, a police cruiser drew up on

a littered street, surrounded by stores so gutted and debased
that they are simply valueless: they are not stores anymore,
they are piles of trash. A twenty-four-year-old black man took
a six-pack of beer from one of them. He saw the cops. He had
been arrested before, so he ran.

A yellow-helmeted cop with a shotgun leaped out of the
cruiser. He aimed the gun with *his kind* of all deliberate
speed and shot the black man dead . . . for a six-pack of
beer! And the spreading pellets from the murderous blast
tore their way into the soft flesh of Joe Bass, Jr., a black shoe-
shine boy, twelve years old, with nothing in his hands. He
was struck in the neck and the thigh and fell bleeding to the
pavement, his eyes open and staring straight ahead, his body
almost finding a restful embrace in the dirty asphalt.

The Newark policeman, his shotgun still at the ready,
turns away from the murdered Billy Furr, the looter of a six-
pack of beer. There is no anguish in his face, his mouth is
relaxed, almost soft as he reaches into the side pocket of his
blue shirt for a cigar. The story is told accurately and
compassionately, even to the point of telling how when little
Joey was struck down fifty sobbing black men and women
tried to get to him, to help him, and were clubbed back by a
small squad of police with rifle butts. But the name of the
murderer in the blue uniform shirt is not reported. And it is
possible he will never be known, and his face will be forgotten, for the police in this country, when they are acting
against the black people, are usually faceless and nameless and
omnipotent, infallible and unpunishable, like Yahweh.

There was the Boston Massacre and there was the Newark Massacre. The last took place yesterday, in our time, in
our country; the men who carried it out bore our faces, the
bullets that found their way anonymously into black bodies
were paid for, in part by us. It is our consciousness, our herit-
age, vibrating in the air we breathe.

Let us examine again the rules we live by . . . the life,

liberty and pursuit of happiness guarantees. These rules say, if these guarantees are not forthcoming . . . "that whenever any form of government shall become destructive of these ends, it is the right of the people to alter or abolish it, and to institute a new government."

Certainly, no one in his right mind will deny that this form of government has been highly destructive to the life, liberty, *et cetera* of the black people. This, above all things, is self-evident. The black people are still in a social, economic, and political bondage. After a great war was fought to free them, they are not free. There is no excuse for the brute fact that our parliamentary system has not been able to bring them into the mainstream of American life. Not only that, their story can only be told in times of upheaval and self-slaughter. And even after these take place, the only comment made on it, or the only ones asked about it, are old crocks like Senator Dirksen, someone who is supremely irrelevant to what is going on, anywhere, and who yet is considered one of the two or three leading spokesmen of our government. All he can say is that we, the whites, are "getting impatient with this disregard of law and order." This fact alone, that Dirksen is speaking for it, shows the complete idiocy and futility of the Congress.

We say over and over again that the solving of the race question will take time, but there is no excuse for this. We establish new forms of government because it took too much time before, in the old form, to resolve an accursed question of human suffering. New governments are not to create a continuation of the same wrongs and social stultifications that made the new form a bloody imperative. We have had long enough . . . enough, enough to see ourselves as white-skinned racists creating and maintaining a society where some get all the good of it while others deeply suffer . . . where the good of one comes out of the evil put upon another . . . where we exist in a prison of our white skin as inescapable as that of our black neighbors. What we do to the black people, daily, makes me want to secede from the white race! It makes me, down deep, hate myself, and my color. All decent whites especially the young whites, abhor having to bear the burden of racist guilt their fathers have placed upon them.

And they hate white racist America and their own fathers for sustaining it, for stealing from them what should have been a birthright of human brotherhood, alienating them from young blacks by white cruelty to them, in their white image. For setting up impassable barriers between young whites and young blacks, areas of suspicion coming from a constant betrayal. They want to clasp hands with the blacks, if only in admiration of the dignity, patience, and restraint they have shown up to this breaking point. If we let them alone they will offer them love and support for their bloody struggle to rise to a level of liberation and privilege which whites accept as due to them by their birth alone.

And we adults: we hate white racist America because it has blocked out of the culture of our time the unfettered expression of the wisdom of a people to whom the meaning of life has had to be privation, suffering and alienation, but who have lived, somehow, with moments of ecstasy, with spurts of infectuous and inexplicable joy. White racist America makes me ashamed of my own country, which not only presents to a vibrant, revolutionary world the complacent facade of a sluttish society whose mass ideal is the unlimited consumption of all possible goods and services . . . but has lost all of its revolutionary virtues in an hour when the darker people are finally climbing into the light, and are forced to seek elsewhere the encouragement which some of our revolutionary fathers meant for us to bestow upon mankind. And in the losing of this revolutionary virtue, we have turned despicably into our opposites and are murdering revolutionaries all over the world.

And all the time we are doing this we are telling the

little white children, and some of the little black children, that Abe Lincoln said in 1848: "Any people anywhere being inclined and having the power, have the right to rise up and shake off the existing government, and form a new one that suits them better. This is a most valuable and sacred right, a right we hope and believe is to liberate the world."

And we are teaching high school students, black and white, that Abe Lincoln, the great emancipator, said, in his First Inaugural Address: "This country, with its institutions, belongs to the people who inhabit it. Whenever they shall grow weary, of the existing government, they can exercise their constitutional right of amending it, or their revolutionary right to dismember, or overthrow it."

They tell us that we have this great and basic right, but if we so much as suggest the use of it, we are punished . . . we are imprisoned. So that it serves as an entrapment, a vicious provocation to smoke out radicals and revolutionaries. Why do they say this . . . why do they so piously quote the forefathers and then blame and hurt people under an unforgivable longevity of oppression . . . obviously getting worse instead of better . . . for trying to act under it?

The United States House of Representatives has just demonstrated its imbecility and outright betrayal of the Bill of Rights, which it has sworn to uphold, by passing a bill which makes traveling from one state to another and saying anything that might be, after the fact, twisted into a connection with a riot, a criminal offense. It carries a fine of ten thousand dollars or imprisonment for five years, or both.

It was written by a white racist from Florida and forced onto the floor by the white racist from Mississippi, who said, the insurrections in the black ghettos were "organized conspiracies backed by the Communists . . . if you vote against this bill, what are you going to say when you go home and meet the policeman and fireman who risked their lives, and in many instances, lost them. . . ." As if it was not already clear that the lawless, conspiratorial, rioting element in the community is the police themselves.

This does not mean that the Southern racist congressmen were responsible for the bill. Charles W. Sandman, Jr., a Republican from New Jersey, was one of its most ardent supporters and said the police in Newark had told him that rioters had crossed the Hudson River in buses, were picked up in cars and taken to the center of Newark, where the trouble occurred. There is no proof in existence that this did occur, while on the other hand it is well known that the police will say anything that will develop their own positions. So the bill was passed by a vote of 347 to 70 . . . and they were not all Southern congressmen who voted for it.

This is how we put off, again and again, truth and resolution for some dishonest and shoddy solution. And then we snivel and hurt the helpless when the chickens come home to roost. It was not outside agitators behind the guns of Newark . . . it could be the inflammatory boasts and texts of our daily education. Now they will have to prevent Thomas Jefferson, in the form of his writings, from crossing state lines, for he said: "What country can preserve its liberties if their rulers are not warned from time to time that this people preserve the spirit of resistance. Let them take arms. . . ."

Or if the agitator from New Jersey crosses the line into Pennsylvania, he will find the Pennsylvania Declaration of Rights already there, saying: "The Community hath an indubitable, inalienable, and indefeasible right to reform, alter or abolish government in such manner as shall be by that community judged most conducive to the public weal."

Henry Clay of Kentucky, the Great Commoner, said: "An oppressed people are authorized, whenever they can, to rise and break their fetters."

John Adams, the second President of the United States, said: "It is an observation of one of the profoundest inquiries into human affairs that a revolution of government is the strongest proof that can be given by a people, of their virtue and good sense."

His son, also a President of the United States, said: "In the abstract theory of our government, the obedience of the citizen is not due to an unconstitutional law: he may lawfully resist its execution."

And Henry D. Thoreau, a good revolutionary, an artist of the revolutionaries, said: "All men recognize the right of revolution, that is the right to refuse allegiance to and to resist, the government where its tyranny or its inefficiency are great and unendurable."

In Maryland its Declaration of Rights reads: "Whenever the ends of government are perverted, and public liberty manifestly endangered, and all other means of redress are ineffectual, the people may, and of right ought to, reform the old or establish a new government; the doctrine of nonresistance against arbitrary power and oppression is absurd, slavish and destructive of the good and happiness of mankind."

General and President U. S. Grant said: "The right of Revolution is an inherent one. When people are oppressed by their government, it is a natural right they enjoy to relieve themselves of the oppression if they are strong enough, either by withdrawing from it, or by overthrowing it and substituting a government more acceptable."

And Emerson, talking of affairs in Kansas, when white settlers in 1856 had to knuckle down to racist tyrants and live like people in the black ghettos today, said:

> I think there never was a people so choked and stultified by forms. We adore the forms of law, instead of making them vehicles of wisdom and justice. Language has lost its meaning in the universal cant. . . . *Representative Government* is really misrepresentative. *Democracy, Freedom,* fine names for an ugly thing. They call it attar of roses and lavender, — I call it bilge water. They call it Chivalry

and Freedom; I call it the stealing of all the earnings of a
poor man and the earnings of his little girl and boy, and the
earnings of all that shall come from him his children's children forever. But this is union and this is Democracy, and
our poor people, led by the nose by these fine words, dance
and sing, ring bells and fire cannon, with every new link
of the chain which is forged for their limbs by the plotters
in the Capital. . . . What are the results of law and Union?
There is no Union. The judges give cowardly interpretation
to the law, in direct opposition to the known foundation
of all law, *that every immoral statute is void!* If that be law,
let the ploughshare be run under the foundations of the
Capitol — and if that be Government, extirpation is the only
cure. I am glad that the terror at disunion and anarchy is
disappearing. . . .

Now I submit that somewhere, every day in this country, some schoolboy is reading about these men; that their
words, revolution and all, are passing into their consciousness. This being undeniably true . . . how can we stop
these dangerous thoughts from crossing state lines, color
lines, or lines of any kind? We could not stop them from
entering the icy legal mind of Mr. Justice Jackson, late of
the Supreme Court, who gave, in 1950, the most concrete
modern juridical opinion of the right of revolution based
on the Declaration of Independence.

. . . we cannot ignore the fact that our own government originated in revolution, and is legitimate only if overthrow by force can sometimes be justified. That circumstances
sometimes justify it is not Communist doctrine, but an old
American belief. The men who led the struggle forcibly to
overthrow lawfully constituted British authority found moral
support by asserting a natural law under which their revolution was justified, and they bravely proclaimed their belief
in the document basic to our freedom. Such sentiments have
also been given ardent and rather extravagant expression by
Americans of undoubted patriotism.

So there it is, deep in the hide of the Republic, and you can talk about it all you want, having a revolution, that is, just as long as it is in a classroom, and you are white. But don't say it, as William Epton did, on the streets of Harlem before a group of silent men, whose eyes have a tiny glow like the stirring of a long-banked fire.

4.

HOGAN'S COURT

THE energy and skill with which the white American liberal and *radical* suppresses his revolutionary morality, and disavows his revolutionary conscience are remarkable. He romantically remembers the great revolutionaries of the past but he cannot produce a contemporary one, here and now, in this country. We have the vote, jobs, money, more than the workingman and the middle class have ever had before. Still we cannot create a third party, a third force, in the form of simple opposition to the twin hypocrisies of the "major" parties. A revolutionary party is out of the question.

We have "democratic" power over our rulers, and yet we have allowed as many of our acknowledged rights and liberties to be taken away from us, by default and indifference, as those the blacks have had denied them by force. We serve cringingly under a Chief Executive as arrogant as Frederick the Great, who also said, "I have come to an agreement with my people. I am to permit them to say whatever they want. And they are to permit me to do whatever I want."

Black people must wonder why, with all this consensus of white liberal power, we stand so silently when we should be heard, so tolerant and objective when we should be fighting mad . . . so frightened and secretive when we should have been rising in righteous power to rebuke and punish those who subvert the rights of man for profit and privilege . . . and doing this so swiftly and totally that no one trying this for the second time would have the smallest chance of escape.

Black people see us truckling to keep the things they smash, to hoard the buildings they burn, to turn a profit on the things they lay waste. They know that we are so far gone that we can no longer redeem ourselves but have to wait for the uprisings of the wretched of the earth to restore our own country to us.

Instead of being grateful for this process we continue to advise them on the ethical way to operate a resistance movement. They must do it strictly in conformity to our morality, with due and reverent respect for all our *things* . . . for our property. We can smash half the world but they cannot smash a window.

Pseudoradicals, pseudorevolutionaries, in answer to queries on how the white radicals should respond to the ghetto rebellions, tell the blacks first that their rebellion was not revolutionary because . . . "not all angry words are revolutionary, nor is every pint of whisky drunk for the cause, even if it is taken from a looted store." They tell the black man not to appear as a "hoodlum" in the national white press and that to flout the white man's morality vis-à-vis his private property degrades a revolutionary into a "criminal." Anyone who does not go into the streets shouting slogans of "justice, compassion and universality," without "disavowing personal advantage" and demonstrating an "outraged sense of justice," is fighting for "fascism or incoherence." Thus it is obvious that many white radicals have already drawn up their defenses against having to participate in slum rebellions.

With the plainness and clarity of an Old Testament prophet, William Epton, a black man, stood at Lenox Ave-

nue and 115th Street, New York City, on July 18, 1964, at
approximately 5 P.M. and made a speech, something he had
done almost every Saturday afternoon that summer. It was a
revolutionary speech.

Epton believes in the right of revolution: that when a
long chain of abuses makes you want to change the government, you should go openly into the streets where the abuses
are being committed, talk to the oppressed people, and make
them realize the truth of what's happening to them, so that
they will be able to "coherently" resist it. Then, Epton believes, you should have an open place where people can go
with their wounds and their complaints and be listened to
and given some hope that during their lifetime justice will
be done them.

Epton is highly indigenous to Harlem, both as a native
son and a revolutionary. He was born there thirty-five years
ago, and he knows the anguish and desperation of that
blasted terrain: black man in Harlem, father a longshore-
man, seven other kids in the family, lived in a tenement
basement one door down from James Baldwin, indigenous
Harlem stock as good as you can get. He went to work at the
age of twelve, shining shoes. On the streets of Harlem all
the time. The streets were different then.

Shining his way up and down Lenox Avenue he saw
the big proud men from the Garvey headquarters, from the
Communist Party offices and meeting rooms, from dozens of
fiery nationalist groups keeping a cheerful buzz in the air
and a bustle of hope. Don't think Harlem never had a revolutionary tradition. Epton grew up in it. There was always
the verbal turbulence of intense political activity, demonstrations, rallies, the magnificent pageantry of Garveyite
parades, black men on horseback with flashing swords and
glittering braid. The black man was brightly visible then
and the streets were his. He did not have to run a gauntlet
of white policemen with hostile questioning eyes and long,

lead-loaded sticks to beat him with each time he walked
from his house to the subway, to a store, to a bar, to church.
The police were not then trained in "counterinsurgency"
and sent in by the swarm, as if to some foreign country on
the edge of upheaval, to put down an always-impending
rebellion.

Epton managed to sweat out an integrated high school
education, after finding out how much he had been short-
changed, educationally, in the ghetto schools. He read his
school texts and Marx with the energy of glut, with the
frenzy of a kid passed in a race, fighting to get up front.
He worked in a casual way in the radical and union movements . . . an experience deeper than he realized. Mostly
he thought of getting out of Harlem and really catching up.
He worked in an aircraft factory in California, was drafted
and went to Korea. (He says he remembered Lenin's saying
that a true revolutionary will not refuse to go into an im-
perialist army.) When he came back he married and went to
live for a while in Haiti, among the end games of imperialism. It was a lesson even Harlem could not teach him: the
absolute total degradation of the human spirit . . . the
meaning of the wretched of the earth. Among these nonre-
ducible elements of human debris his consciousness took the
final and irrevocable step into an existence completely dom-
inated by a revolutionary purpose.

He went back to Harlem to give its people some form
of political coherence, to try to make at least one part of
them whole. He had a discipline and a theory he felt would
defeat racism and defend the people of the ghetto from their
enemies. He wanted to bring the whole struggle into the
open, to get away from the paralysis of guilt and conspiracy
that American radicals too often have, which drives them
to practice forms of political duplicity which almost always
taint their ultimate aim, no matter how lofty it may be. He
was the Vice President of the Progressive Labor Party; he
ran an office to recruit members and sympathizers to fill a

political need. Rent strikes would be organized, traffic lights put on dangerous corners, landlords who act toward their tenants like the wardens at Buchenwald were to be punished by the enforcement of the laws on the books against them.

A day in the life of Harlem is enough to convince most Americans that there are no answers to this degradation in any present political apparatus. It has been a sociological disaster area for generations, and it is getting worse at a frenzied rate. There are certain fixed conditions that everyone knows about. Five hundred thousand black people in one of the most congested areas in the world, with one hospital, grossly inferior schools, the highest rents and the worst buildings, the highest prices for the worst food, the highest rate of unemployment, the lowest grade of service from public agencies, and lately a refusal from the Congress of the United States to seat the Congressman the people in Harlem elected by an overwhelming majority. These, and other visible human indignities, have become the standard description of the Harlem area.

Epton's office at 336 Lenox Avenue became a waiting room for the walking wounded of Harlem. It was a bare, ugly, wasteland place with an oily, splintery floor, a buckling tin roof, frayed with rust and the smell of long human defeat. The doorway at the street level had a long past as a fragile shelter for winos, addicts, and the hopelessly sad. Epton went there every day with a white shirt and tie, as happily as if he were reporting to a major office in the Ford Foundation.

I knew the place well and have sat there for hours listening to stories of injury and brutalization, to threats of violence and revenge. The most common complaint was of the brutality of the police, of being picked up on suspicion, mauled and locked in a cell for weeks, and then being let go without a trial, or without a conviction. When the suspect got out, he had lost his job. Epton talked to everyone that

came in, without concealment, or political hocus-pocus. It
was a free place. It was the bottom.

Shortly after he got there the police sent in an agent,
Adolph Hart. He was what Malcolm X used to call "a
Negro." A police school rookie, his duty was to listen, to
entrap, and destroy Epton and the Progressive Labor Movement. What he told Epton was that he had to join a militant
organization, and Epton took him in on good faith. This
was in November of 1963. He accompanied Epton on speaking engagements and rapidly became more radical than all
the rest. On July 18, when Epton made his speech, Hart
helped set up the ladder, the American flag, and the microphone.

From the day of Hart's entrance into the group it became impossible to know exactly what was said or what was
meant by the whole Harlem P.L.M. operation. Hart became
such a provocateur that he had to be constantly curbed and
admonished and was finally expelled for his absolutely insane militancy. The use of a police spy to obtain evidence is
as valid as torture to gain a confession. They will say anything. You never knew where P.L.M. left off and the New
York Bureau of Special Services began. That same year there
was a police agent in CORE, NAACP and every other civil
rights organization, feeding maggot-like on the suppurating
wound of the black oppressed.

But the tiny malice of one agent was nothing compared
to the mass invasion of Harlem that spring of 1964 by white
mercenaries, in uniform and in disguise: an invasion described by Police Commissioner Murphy as "wall-to-wall
cops." Murphy described his method of law enforcement as
"the substitution of the show of force for the actual use of
force" as if you can ever have one without the other. Cops
stood in quartets, swinging their clubs on every corner and
walked their beats, four abreast. These were not the familiar
fat old hacks, rump-sprung and beefy from riding around in

squad cars. They were a white elite corps, suburban bred, all over six feet tall, "trained in judo," and organized into a paramilitary Tactical Police Force. Then there were cops disguised as winos, as addicts, as homosexuals in drag, as cab-drivers, social workers, data-taking sociologists. They came into Harlem like swarms of locusts, like the plagues of Egypt. It was as if Harlem had just lost a long and bloody war with the men in blue uniforms and were being occupied. There was no retreat, no escape from their infuriating presence. All day and all night racing squad cars made the air hideous with their sirens' indescribable din, a hoarse, nerve-shatter-ing retch, like a giant stomach pump. Fire trucks staged "drill" with open throttles several times a day, which every-one felt was in preparation for turning their hoses, South-ern-style, against the guts of demonstrators.

The press began to create the monstrous image of a Harlem Mau Mau which was tearing up subways, raping white women, and stomping white men to death. It easily supplied the New York police with the moral justification that their subjugation of Harlem with force and violence was putting down "racial" turbulence of a Hitlerite charac-ter, not only anti-white, but virulently anti-Semitic.

The residents of Harlem stood dazed and mute for the most part in the face of this onslaught. If they defended those attacked by the police they were said to be defending racism.

Week in and week out Epton flayed them raw, running the tightrope of permissible abuse. A policeman, off-duty, but still a killer, shot another black boy, fifteen years old and small for his age. He came running belligerently (the police say he had a knife in his hand) out of an apartment house. Thomas Gilligan, a six-foot white police lieutenant, drew his gun and killed him in "self defense."

Hordes of psychologists, legal experts, and "concerned citizens" have been probing the minds of radicals and black people for most of this uneasy generation, trying to find out why they are "alienated," why they are hostile, why they are "violent." None of them ever wants to look into the mind of a cop like Thomas Gilligan and find out why . . . what compulsion of duty, training, standing orders, or routine police practice forced him to pump bullets into the body of a small fifteen-year-old boy running at him, or to join with other men in blue in beating kids with clubs while they are lying prone on the street with handcuffs on. There was a secret Grand Jury investigation of Gilligan, but as everyone expected, he got off, and only a small section of the testimony was ever released to the public.

Epton felt that this killing, the eighth fatal police shooting of black or Puerto Rican citizens since November of 1963 was "the ultimate insult to the black people of this community." On July 18, two days after the incident, he was still seething with a very human rage. He stood up at the regular Saturday street meeting, and he lost his cool at the sight of the usual police standing there in the Harlem Street . . . waiting for him to become the real, and punishable, criminal of the Gilligan killing . . . waiting to leap at him at the first sign of blood . . . which was to be his own . . . all the black people were bleeding a little at the death of schoolboy James Powell. Epton pointed at the agents and began to talk:

> I see a couple of stooges in the audience. A couple of them came up to see me at our headquarters one day, but I'll tell you about that some other time. But I see them in the audience and I'll tell them right now that we're going to have a demonstration and we don't say it's going to be peaceful because the cops have declared war on the people of Harlem and. . . .

Here one excited cop reached in his pocket and turned up the volume of his recorder. It was too loud then, and he lost some of the speech. He adjusted it, and it caught this:

No country or people in the world that have had war declared on them have not declared war on their enemy. They declared war on us, and we should declare war on them, and every time they kill one of us, damn it, we'll kill one of them, and we should start thinking that way now.

He lashed out at the press for their Mau Mau slander. He called the police gangsters, crooks, thieves, and murderers. He told of the time when a few mothers were picketing for a stoplight in front of a school and one hundred armed policemen were stationed secretly in the basement of the school in case the mothers "got out of hand." Unconsciously he began to paraphrase one of the great emancipatory polemics of all time, *State and Revolution,* something professors teach in political science classes every semester. It sounds different in the sullen streets, when they can hide cops in the basements of schools to attack mothers. He said:

That shows you how this system is interwoven . . . because you must understand that when they set up a state, they set up all the apparatus to protect and save that state. They set up the courts; they set up the police; they set up the army; they set up an educational system; they set up the newspaper; they set up all the apparatus to brainwash, and to keep up the subjugation. If we're going to be free, and we will not be fully free until we smash this state completely and totally. Destroy and set up a new state of our own choosing and of our own liking.

And in the process of smashing this state, we're going to have to kill a lot of these cops, a lot of their judges, and we'll have to go up against their army. We'll organize our own militia and our own army. If we don't do it, brothers, you'll be subjugated, we'll be kept in chains for another two or three hundred years. Think about it, because no people in this world have ever achieved independence and freedom through the ballot or having it legislated to them. All the people in this world who are free got their freedom through struggle and through revolution. That's the only way to gain Freedom.

Hart, the police spy dancing attendance on Bill, helped take down the flag, the ladder, and the microphone. The people drifted off to another meeting, or a bar, knowing that what they had just heard was not a threat, or a call to action, or a categorical imperative of any sort, but a great prophecy, like Jeremiah's, or John Brown's saying on his way to the gallows that he knew that the sins of this guilty land of slave owners could only be purged by blood. Did John Brown's speech start the Civil War?

In another part of Harlem, 7th Avenue and 125th Street, CORE was having a far more successful rally. This ended with a march to the 28th Precinct and a sit-down demanding the arrest of Gilligan. A Lieutenant Pendergast came out of the station house with a bull horn. He pointed it at policemen guarding wooden barriers and bellowed, "Get the niggers!" The police then charged the unarmed demonstrators with swinging clubs. This was the beginning of the Harlem riot of 1964.

There have been bigger and bloodier riots since this one, but something about this one needs to be carefully pondered. One of the most frightening aspects of the 1967 upheavals was that they produced no real dialogue between the black and the white. The embattled black made no gestures toward bargaining, making a peace. When it ended, the races were farther apart than ever.

Sartre understands this in his marvelous introduction to Fanon's book, *The Wretched of the Earth*. Speaking to all whites, he illuminates and foretells what will happen:

> After a few steps in the darkness you will see strangers gathered around a fire; come close and listen, for they are talking of the destiny they will mete out to your trading centers and to the hired soldiers who defend them. They will see you, perhaps, but they will go on talking among them-

selves, without even lowering their voices. This indifference
strikes home: their fathers, shadowy creatures, *your creatures,* were but dead souls; you it was who allowed them
glimpses of light, to you only did they dare speak, and you
did not bother to reply to such zombies. Their sons ignore
you; a fire warms them and sheds light around them, and
you have not lit it. Now, at a respectful distance, it is you
who will feel furtive, nightbound and perished with cold.
Turn and turn about; in these shadows from whence a new
dawn will break, it is you who are the zombies.

One of the lessons taught by the Harlem riots is that if
you try to solve its tensions, within it, and in an orderly and
meaningful way, you will get blamed for it, as Epton did.

During the riot Epton and his organization held an
open meeting at their headquarters and hammered out a
ten-point program to demand of the city at a march and
demonstration that coming Saturday. Gilligan was to be arrested and prosecuted for first-degree murder; a people's
Grand Jury was to be convened to investigate police brutality against the black and Puerto Rican citizens; the jury
should listen to everyone with a protest; its transcripts were
to be made public; indictments against brutal policemen
would be drawn from their findings if the evidence demanded it; the people should be allowed to meet in the
streets without police harassment; the constitutional rights
of self defense would be respected; all people who had been
beaten, arrested, and wrongly detained by the police would
be compensated; all extra police would be withdrawn from
Harlem; the city would permit citizens living in buildings
where there were gross violations of the housing laws to
withhold their rents until the infractions were corrected. It
was also voted to get out a "wanted" flyer on Thomas Gilligan. It read, "Wanted for Murder. Gilligan the Cop."

Thoreau once pointed out that radicals often "keep the
law when the government breaks it." This was the only

meeting of its kind in Harlem at this time, the only group
of people not showing panic, submission, and retreat in the
face of gross provocation and injury toward *them*. The
backwash of the three days' rioting had brought into Harlem
the now familiar retaliators — thousands of police with a
staggering variety of pistols, submachine guns, and bazookas
to occupy the black community, ostensibly to prevent any
repetition of the riot, actually to cow them into total submission. It seemed essential that Harlem should show its black
brothers everywhere that it could no longer be frightened
into silence and defeat. Epton's group put out a leaflet:
*Demonstration to Protest Police Brutality in Harlem. Come
to the People's Trial of Gilligan the Cop. Saturday, July 25,
116th and Lenox Avenue.*

This triggered a long series of moves, as intricate as a
chess game, continuing with a single purpose, not only for
days and weeks, but for over a year. Its purpose was to blame
the riots on a single man, on a radical political concept and
thus absolve the city, the country, the system, and tyranny
itself from all culpability.

This was carried out by the office of the District Attorney of Manhattan. In an extremely laudatory article in the
New York Times Magazine, the office of District Attorney
Frank Hogan is called, admiringly, "A Ministry of Justice."
Apparently justice no longer resides in the courts themselves,
where a man can face his accusers and appeal to a jury of
his peers. "Hogan's office determines whether accused people
are guilty or not. . . . Once the D.A. decides you are guilty
of a felony, you are. As of June 23rd [1967], the office has
prosecuted to a conclusion this year, 2,182 people accused
of a felony. Seven of them, one third of one percent, have
been acquitted. . . ." The Supreme Court of the United
States operates on the assumption that we have an adversary
system of law, wherein a man comes innocent to his day in
court and the burden of proof is on the prosecutor's shoul-

ders. "But in New York what we really have is an admin-
istrative system where the important decisions are taken in
the prosecutor's office."

Directly after Epton's meeting, agents began reporting
to Hogan's office. An injunction was drawn, forbidding all
protest meetings in Harlem, naming as particular defendants
Epton; Conrad Lynn, then head of the Freedom Now party;
Jesse Gray, the organizer of rent strikes and "all other persons whomsoever, known or unknown active in their behalf,
or in concord with them. . . ." They were prevented from
"in any manner or any means . . . assembling, gathering
together, marching, demonstrating, or acting in concert in
the public area in the borough of Manhattan, City of New
York, bounded by 110 St. in the south, 155 St. in the north,
Franklin Delano Roosevelt Drive on the east, and the Hudson River on the west . . ."

The injunction was based on the tapes made at Epton's
speech. District Attorney Hogan had made a transcript and
released it to the press. He said that he was asking for the
injunction "to prevent the defendants from violating section 161 of the penal law of the state of New York." That
section states that anyone who by word of mouth advises or
teaches the necessity of overthrowing organized government
is guilty of criminal anarchy. The implication was clear that
Epton was already considered guilty and anyone talking like
him, or joining with him, would be considered to be teaching the overthrow of the government and punished accordingly. Furthermore, the persons named in the injunction
were ordered to appear in court the following week to show
cause why their silence should not be made permanent.

At this point, thirty civil-rights leaders, said to represent
seventy-six Harlem organizations, met with Mayor Wagner
to discuss the demonstration and the injunction. Presumably
they were informed that the injunction might be made "permanent," but there is no recorded moment of shock any-

where among them. It is staggering to note that a whole community could be thus singled out and told that it was shut off *permanently* from every guarantee of the Constitution and the Bill of Rights. I say *every guarantee* because if it is legal to exclude a whole section of this country's people from any part of its legal rights, it is legal to exclude them from them all.

It would seem that the threat of this injunction alone would have compelled the civil-rights leaders sitting with the Mayor to call out every single member of their purported seventy-six organizations. But these civil-rights leaders seemed to know it would only be used against bad guys like Epton and Jesse Gray and those under their influence. Perhaps they were formally reassured about this. In any case they showed no real concern that such an injunction, with its brazen claim of permanency backed up by a ruthless police power, was itself overthrowing, with force and violence, the government.

Performing dutifully on cue, the leaders held a "unity" meeting, on Saturday, a few hours before the demonstration announced by Epton. Epton was invited and quickly learned that the sole purpose of the gathering was to get him to call off his march. Epton decided he was going to march anyway, as a token defiance, in spite of their opposition and the injunction. At the announced time he and his lawyer, Conrad Lynn, and William MacAdoo took the dangerous walk down their home streets. Because these three men were walking, there were hundreds of policemen alerted, guarding the subway exits, stopping people from coming out of shops and restaurants, stationed on roofs with pointed tommy guns. When Epton and Lynn reached 168th Street, where the march was supposed to begin, they were put under arrest by a police captain, a Negro. They were whisked downtown and charged with disorderly conduct and unlawful assembly. Their arrest was illegal, and they were released, because in the haste to stifle them and the banned march, they had been taken into custody before the injunction had been even signed by the proper authority. However, the police had learned to their satisfaction that Epton was considered expendable by the other leaders, and they had him isolated and vulnerable.

The demonstration Epton had planned while the injunction was on was, I believe, the breaking point of the civil-rights movement. After this came its decline and the decisions of the black people to go it alone. In those climactic days during the Harlem riots, the eyes of the nation were on them; the now fixed pattern of police suppression was obvious. The black people of Harlem are the most sophisticated, the most rights-conscious in the world. If thousands of people by merely leaving their homes could have stood in the streets of Harlem, calling out for simple justice and demonstrating their constitutional right to meet, at any time, and under any conditions, to protest for redress of their grievances, it would have had an impact far greater than any number of catch-all and contrived "marches," which become entities in themselves and political dead ends.

The time to demonstrate is when you are forbidden to, at the place where a long chain of abuses cries out for correction, and for the punishment of those creating injustices and oppression. And what of those whites who march by the thousands and then by hundreds of thousands in protest when they are protected by the law . . . when they have permission. Don't they realize that the mere granting of permission demonstrates their ineffectuality? If they had assembled by the thousands, by the hundreds of thousands on the banned streets of Harlem this act would have had some revolutionary meaning here and in every other American ghetto. They knew about it; the press had been following the whole injunction process hour by hour, almost minute by minute. But the whites stayed away.

This classic moment of hesitation or indifference, this failure of nerve which seems to be so curiously embedded in the consciousness of the white liberal and pacifist, who are deterred by their "scruples" from acting other than in nonviolent ways, was an enormously costly one for them. The "march" next time will be between the cops, the troopers, and the National Guard, dug in and firing on one side of the street, and the besieged black tenements on the other. The black people are already asking where the liberals were when the guns were going off massacring women and children in Newark and Detroit. Black people for years have been told by whites that it was the height of bravery and effectuality to put their black bodies in front of the oppressor and his clubs, whips, hoses, and guns. Now is the chance for the whites to be the sacrificial lambs and to cheerfully soak up the lead in their own white bodies, singing, "We shall overcome someday."

On August 3 Hogan's court assembled a Grand Jury as remote from being Epton's peers as the British House of Lords, downtown, on alien ground and far from the conflicts of Harlem. It was a panel of twenty-three hand-picked, middle-class defenders. Their addresses were Park Avenue, Central Park West, and Lincoln Towers. It was unabashedly blue ribbon. Ten were owners or officers of corporations; two were stock brokers; there was an advertising executive and a retired real estate salesman, and six highly paid professionals. They were so alien, so heartbreakingly alien to Bill Epton and the meaning of his life. In a city of one million Puerto Ricans, of two million union members, how come none of these were on the panel?

The fear and trembling of the New York press, which constantly raised a specter of a lawless community inflamed into running amok by a subversive political party, the fear and trembling in the judge who signed away the Constitution from Harlem to silence Epton, the knowledge that it is "standard operating procedure" for the trial court to assume that the guilt of the accused has already been infallibly determined in the DA's office, met sympathetic vibrations in this Blue Ribbon Jury, and two days after convening they indicted Epton for Criminal Anarchy: the useful section 160–161 of New York's penal law. From then on to his trial he was never away from pursuing and observing detectives . . . the P.L.M. headquarters was under tight surveillance, and the police opened a temporary office directly across from the Harlem P.L.M. center.

The speed and ease with which the indictment of Epton came off was then threatened, however, by a finding by the FBI that the riot was "a senseless attack on all constituted authority without direct purpose or object. . . . There was no systematic planning or organization." Police Commissioner Murphy then announced that the FBI report "coincides with our findings." Something had to be done to sustain the position of Frank S. Hogan and his infallible Ministry of Justice that Epton and Progressive Labor had triggered the riot, after arming Harlem with guns and Molotov cocktails, and that Epton had led the uprising as the general of a genuine insurrection.

In what seems to be a desperate attempt to get evidence other than that offered by police agents paid by the week with a guaranteed pension and fringe benefits, nearly fifty people were subpoenaed and brought before the wearers of the blue ribbons. They were picked up in dawn raids: the police, sometimes in squads of eight and ten, entering their apartments without warrants, ransacking them, and acting roughly toward all the occupants in a kind of deliberate terror. None talked, although all were threatened with arrest, sentences, and fines. Thirteen were later indicted for criminal contempt and taken into custody with their hands manacled behind their backs. Among the fifty picked up for questioning were members of SNCC, and the student May

Second Movement . . . the net was wide and it was made plain that any known connection with P.L.M. was a priori guilt in the Grand Jury room.

Epton's own consciousness of guilt was nonexistent. The people he was talking to around Harlem said they knew something was wrong when a man that kills a boy gets off, and the man who complains about it is arrested and put on trial. With the indictment of criminal anarchy still over his head, he filed papers to run for state senator in the November 1965 elections. With very little trouble his candidacy was endorsed by the signatures of more than 6,400 voters of his district, and he was duly certified by the Board of Elections as a legitimate candidate. He campaigned vigorously on a socialist platform. "The rich are not fit to govern the poor. They are not fit to run anything, for their self-interests always come before the needs of the people. . . ." On election day it was discovered that in fifty Harlem election districts, where the voters were sure to be black, the voting machines did not have his name on them. Where there was an even balance of races, the name was on, but the levers were missing. In white neighborhoods all was in perfect order. Even so, Epton got over a thousand votes in all-white districts. An examiner on the Board of Elections admitted that Epton had a legitimate complaint, but this crime against Epton and the democratic process never met any further rebuke.

The time bomb wound up for Epton in the police tapes of July 18, 1964, finally exploded in November, 1965. His trial was a complete non sequitur. He stood in court as a revolutionary socialist. He had never denied this. This was his crime, as his defense was the right of revolution. He was tried for being a "criminal anarchist," and faced a possible penalty of seventeen years in jail and $12,000 in fines. It was admitted by the court itself that he had not committed a single *behavioral* act of lawbreaking. The judge at the trial ruled that it could not be proved that he had participated in the riot, or that he was even present during the disturbances. Nor was there any proof given that anyone who heard him speak, or received a copy of one of his leaflets, participated in the disturbance. But the prosecutor, Joseph Phillips, said, "There is violence in the defendant's mind . . . directed against the state, or overthrowing the state."

Anarchy is a word foreign to us . . . it is almost always called "criminal anarchy," as atheism is called "godless atheism." If you call a man a *revolutionary,* he becomes indigenous. If they had tried Epton for being a revolutionary it would have been a whole new battlefield. Everybody with the slightest interest knew that Epton's party, the Progressive Labor Movement, has all the abhorrence every socialist group has of what is called "anarchy" — planlessness, leaderlessness. P.L.M. is programmed to the teeth. Sometimes they become strangled in the looping proliferation of their programming.

It seemed stupid on the state's part to try Epton for being an anarchist: It seems to mean that the state has so little respect for his legal rights that they do not have to be rational with him. Actually it is very clever because it is saying: You radicals and revolutionaries can bring up all the libertarian defenses you can find, and the cleverest and most dedicated lawyers, but we have the advantage of choosing the battlefield, and we will always select one on which your arguments and your citations from the Supreme Court and your hopeful evocations of bloody victories over benightedness and the dark are simply irrelevant to the case.

The court would not even let one of Epton's defense witnesses, a professor from Princeton, tell the jury what the technical differences were between a communist and an anarchist. In Epton's "criminal" speech, he said, ". . . and in the process of smashing this state. . . ." Professor Hugh Wilson, the throttled witness, wanted to define the word

state, as meant by the defendant — in the Marxian sense as
the whole political system that was oppressing his people
and himself. This was denied by the court because they had
chosen the crime he was supposed to have committed.

Epton was removed from reality and meaning by being
tried for four crimes: For *conspiracy* to commit riot . . .
when the principal evidence was that he made a speech to a
small group of anonymous people on a public street corner
in the high light of a summer afternoon. To *conspire* in
the dictionary is "to combine privately for an unlawful purpose," something that cannot stand the light of the sun. At
least two policemen known to Epton were listening as he
spoke. They always listened when he spoke. He said, "I see
a couple of stooges in the audience." What kind of a conspiracy is this, when you tell policemen what you are going
to do?

The crime of *riot,* the second count against him, was
dismissed by the judge because there was no evidence to
connect the defendant with any breach of the peace. Ration-
ally, if the defendant had no connection with a riot, he
could not have "conspired" to commit it. So the judge, un-
like the wiser ones, or at least, the more honest ones who
dismissed Theodore Parker's case, as we shall see, because
of a flaw in the indictment, tinkered a bit with the indictment, during the trial, so as to make the crime fit the punishment a little better. It was changed to read that Epton had
conspired to participate in a riot "which *would* disturb the
public peace" . . . if it had ever happened. A motion to
dismiss was denied.

Crimes three and four involved penal law 160–161,
which is defined as covering criminal anarchy. "The doctrine
that organized government should be overthrown by force
and violence, or by assassination of the executive head or of
any of the executive officers of the government, or by any

unlawful means." This statute was passed in New York state in 1902 in reaction to the assassination of President McKinley. It was used only once before the Epton case to convict a communist, Benjamin Gitlow, forty years ago. The United States Supreme Court has ruled, over and over again, that Federal legislation, such as the Smith Act, has preempted state control of acts covered by penal law 161, and the state may not act against this type of alleged crime. It seems plain, that an appeal to the high court would reverse this case, but the state went ahead anyway, to hurt and harass Epton, in violation of its own law, as other states will now go ahead with their homegrown sedition acts to put down radicals in spite of and in defiance of the highest court in the land.

In the prosecutor's summary, it was conceded that there was no danger posed by Epton that the government was going to be overthrown, or any officer of the state, even a police officer, was going to be assassinated . . . but there were dire thoughts against the state in the defendant's mind.

Arthur Markewich — he was hardly a "judge" as defined — charged the jury with his thoughts and conclusions as a dead battery is charged from a live electrical socket. He told them to think of what was in Epton's mind. "The biggest question in this case is the intent with which the defendant performed various acts, issued various writings, and made various statements." Each time Arthur Markewich referred to the crime he said "overthrow of the government," without specifying that it referred to the state of New York. He said flatly there was no proof of "advocacy of assassination," but said that the jury didn't have to think about that because there was enough in finding advocacy of force and violence. The crime was, the judge said, "advocating the taking of action which would lead to the overthrow of the government by force and violence."

He did not tell the jury that according to his own

ground rules, standard American judicial procedure, the crime of riot cannot be committed without the agreement of three or more persons, or that a conspiracy charge merges with the charge of riot and one cannot stand without the other . . . he merely changed the indictment creating a new and different crime. He said that what was "communism" and what was "anarchism" was "peculiarly a question for the jury to decide and no expert can be heard to testify on this subject in this particular situation." He allowed the jury to determine the issue of whether a clear and present danger existed without telling them, in all fairness and justice, that Epton's language, in order to be legally dangerous, had to advocate immediate revolutionary action, and there had to be a danger that action would result, and that the group addressed was in a position of such strength that danger to the state could be reasonably apprehended. The First Amendment is considered of such overwhelming importance that when these rights are at stake there cannot be a conviction for conspiracy unless all the clear and present danger elements for overthrow are present . . . which are, a group of overwhelming size, with full cohesiveness and an orientation toward action. The court record of the Epton case shows no evidence that his words were directed toward the government of the state of New York, or that there was any danger of a rebellion taking place. There was no admission by Arthur Markewich that all of Epton's acts were protected by the First Amendment, and the making of speeches, however insulting, is a time-honored means of expressing opinions protected by the State and Federal Constitutions.

The blue-ribbon jury got the charge, the message, that Bill Epton, a black man, a poor man, and a communist, had therefore no rights the court had to respect. He was found guilty on this statute of 1902: it could have been the Dred Scott Decision of 1856. His sentence was trifling in compari-

son to the ordeals through which he and his comrades had
already passed, and mild enough to curb the outpouring of
public sympathy which might have come from a harsher
punishment.

After serving nearly three months of his one-year sentence he was released on $25,000 bail, pending the appeal
yet to be heard. The usual practice is to allow a defendant
to remain out of jail on a certificate of reasonable doubt in
a case like this. Epton, but for the hard work of his lawyers,
could have served his entire sentence and thus made his appeal useless. In every aspect of this case, it is true, he was
treated differently from white defendants.

But when he got back to Harlem he was treated the
same as ever . . . respectfully. And he resumed the struggle
as if nothing bad had happened to him.

> It was our belief that we had a right to be communists
> and tell the people about it. And the people in the commu-
> nity didn't shy away from us, they weren't afraid of us, and
> they asked us to keep it up and hoped that at some future
> point they would be able to join us, or work with us. And it
> only proved that if you are honest in your approach to peo-
> ple . . . don't lie to them, tell them what you believe in
> and do it in a principled way . . . maybe they won't join
> you . . . maybe they're afraid to join you . . . but they
> do have respect for you. And we do have a tremendous
> amount of respect and love in the community. Because we
> have respect for people and we always defend them. And we
> have love for them too and people recognize this. So we will
> go on and do all these things that we can do till we hope
> there's a revolution in this country and we do have socialism.

The lessons provided by the Epton Case are clear. Now
all radicals know that police somewhere are winding up a
time-bomb tape for them, and that there will be an explosion
that will have to be survived. Epton confessed, like Theo-

dore Parker, more than the government could prove, which was that nothing is more dangerous to poverty, racism, and brutal police suppression than a black man with a political theory . . . the right of revolution.

John Brown came to Boston, in early 1855, after having killed, in Pottawatamie, Kansas, members of a county court and a Grand Jury, which was indicting for treason the leaders of the Free Soil Party, as revolutionary in its time and place as the P.L.M. is today. He was respectfully and admiringly entertained by Parker, Emerson, and Thoreau. When it was learned that a U.S. marshal from Kansas, with a murder warrant for the old man, was in hot pursuit, Theodore Parker said this to Judge Thomas Russell, who was concealing John Brown in his house:

> My dear Judge — If John Brown falls into the hands of the marschall from Kansas, he is sure either of the gallows or of something yet worse. If I were in that position, I should shoot dead any man who arrested me for those alleged crimes; then I would be tried by a Massachusetts jury and acquitted.

But the courts no longer give the radical the chance to put the country, or the society, on trial in his stead. They have become impossibly debauched . . . they are slipping backward into Star Chambers, they are not as liberal as those of a hundred years ago. They are bad battlegrounds. And the lawyers, even the best of them, are still officers of the court, still play the game according to the accepted rules, and the only rules the state will now accept are those which support the society as it is, and as they want it to continue.

The black people in the ghetto watched the Epton case. They knew as well as the Doctrinaire pseudorevolutionaries that Epton was acting with the ultimate revolutionary virtue and morality, had gone there with clean hands and a stainless record, with theories, with "programs," with a record of direct involvement with the so-called democratic process.

None of this worked for him. He was still guilty, of being black.

They saw him being forced to play the game the conqueror lays out for him, the legal dodging and twisting to squirm out of a trap holding you in an area you cannot bear being part of . . . being innocent of what they accused him of, and guilty of what they didn't dare accuse him of. They knew that if Epton had been provided with some ground on which to take an honest stand he would have cried out, as his party newspaper did, that he could not be accused of overthrowing a "lawful government" because the government they were referring to was not "lawful" and that in a free court he could have said, as Henry Thoreau did, "The only government that I recognize . . . is that power that establishes justice in the land, never that which establishes injustice."

With these hidden continuities in mind, these defeats and frauds, the black people are no longer listening and talking in the streets, using their "inalienable rights" to work for change. They are getting ready to go for broke. Since William Epton's day in court an enormous gulf has opened up between a government which is supposed to be of laws, and not of men, and a people it despises. I doubt that they are studying Epton's revolutionary methods, which are, in the long run, a process of universal consent. They are reading Robert Williams, the black philosopher of the minority revolution. The swift unexpectedness, the spontaneity, the anonymity of Newark and Detroit, those qualities which the whites find so mindless, has proved this.

Robert Williams says:

> The new concept of revolution is to huddle as close to the enemy as possible so as to neutralize his modern and fierce weapons. The new concept creates conditions that involve the total community, whether they want to be involved or not. It sustains a state of confusion and destruction of

property. It dislocates the organs of harmony and order and reduces central power to the level of a helpless, sprawling octopus. During the hours of day, sporadic rioting takes place and massive sniping. Night brings all-out warfare, organized fighting, and unlimited terror against the oppressor and his forces. Such a campaign will bring an end to oppression and social injustice in the U.S.A. in less than ninety days and create the basis for the implementation of the U.S. Constitution with liberty and justice for all.

5.

NEGROES WITH GUNS

ROBERT WILLIAMS lived in a little town in North Carolina called Monroe. It was deeply racist, and the Klan had one of their biggest regional headquarters there. In spite of this Williams was able to organize the black people to resist, as our revolutionary fathers resisted, the oppression of white racists. They were jailed, strafed, shot at, and subjected to every assault with which every genuine resistance movement has been met, and they held together.

They held together in such a way that Williams began to believe, back there in 1959, that not only the black people would follow a leader that resisted racism by force and insurrection, if necessary, but that the American whites, including the Southern American whites, would respect the blacks more, and relinquish their power more easily and peacefully, if the black men fought them hand to hand for it.

Williams is now an exile, first in Cuba, now in China, but his personality is so powerful, so prophetical that some of the more sophisticated commentators on the current black insurrections blame him for them, even at that remove. He was right about many things, and I hope he was right about the American whites.

We are so disconnected with one another, we whites, in the simple parallel contacts of our daily living, and in all our major emotional relationships, that even our art has become an expression of this. I believe that this alienation does not exist among the oppressed; that they are members of each other far more than we believe. I think they cling to and nourish many hidden continuities that we do not understand. I think one of these continuities is what happened to Robert Williams. I think he is still moving and shaking them.

Williams had been in the Marines. He had come back to Monroe, the place of his birth, to get that shock of recognition that comes so powerfully to Negroes returning to the South after being in the service. There is a recognition that municipal government there is a military one along the lines of troops occupying and controlling an enemy or colonial people. It is easy, once the military posture has been drilled into a man, to understand that the Southern policeman is more a soldier, operating under forms of law so illogically and capriciously personal that they are an insult to any honest legal intelligence.

Just as slavery was a state of war, segregation is. Courts and due process merely validate police action based on brute force. When a white claims injury from a Negro, he does not go before the Grand Jury to give testimony and make his complaint. A police officer usually does this. Trial juries are not asked by the prosecution to make a judgment on the basis of physical evidence submitted in open court but on the basis of information given by the police officer who states the case for the prosecution. The policeman does not present the evidence . . . he *is* the evidence, its total personification. In this way, it is the police power itself that is always on trial in the courts. To go against this evidence is dangerous, even treasonable to the white community. It has to be upheld.

Williams, rightly angered by this, cast around for some elementary form of resistance — some way of bearing witness to it. The first thing to do was to talk about it, for if it is never admitted, as it never has been by the white South, then it cannot be corrected. The NAACP, for all its short-comings, has carried the enormous burden of Negro wrongs for many years and been incessantly and repetitively vocal about it. So to call local and perhaps national attention to the plight of a segregated town in what has always been regarded as the most liberal Southern state, North Carolina, Williams re-formed a defunct branch of the NAACP. At first he tried to get the more successful Negroes to function with him, but when that failed he was able to recruit domestic workers, the underemployed and underpaid, the real masses of the region.

Monroe, North Carolina, with a present population of some 12,000, has been a railroad town since 1860. The Negro population was once employed by the railroads, but with the decline in rail transportation all over the country, they were thrown out of work. Industrial developments were enticed in from the North and forced to sign contracts barring Negroes from any jobs above the menial. There are no unions in Union County, of which Monroe is the shire town. Government development funds have been poured in and whites, from as far away as Texas, imported and trained for government-supported jobs. Local Negroes were not employed, and the racial employment pattern so dear to the white South has been faithfully preserved.

With the dues-paying membership almost totally made up of domestics and part-time workers, Williams was able to create a strong and ethically responsive branch of the NAACP. He happens to be a poet, as, oddly enough, were the other American prophets, Garrison, John Quincy Adams, Whittier, Thoreau, and Emerson. Using his exuberant creativity as a wedge, he was able to obtain the use of the Monroe Public Library for himself and his talent, and then parlay this into its desegregation. This first victory was very important to Williams, and a small, interracial Unitarian Fellowship backed him in this move. He joined it and there found a friendly, even brotherly response to his talent and his ideas.

His next task was tougher: to desegregate the local swimming pool, built and operated by government funds. Here he ran into one of the basic white Southern insanities, that proximity to Negroes in water is a major taboo. He decided to allow for this, merely asking the city officials that the pool be set aside for one day a week for Negro children. This was turned down with the argument that they would have to drain the pool directly after and fill it with clean water, and this would be too expensive. This was the final answer and a very exacerbating one to the Negroes of Monroe. Two of their children had just been drowned swimming in a fast creek nearby, the only source of refreshment in the summer heat. Memory of this was one of the elements turning the armed Negroes in the streets of Newtown (the Negro section) on the Sunday afternoon of August 27, 1961, into a mob as reckless and explosive as the one surging around the courthouse.

Pecksniffian liberals in the North, resting after the desegregation decision of 1954, did not seem to realize that white Southern resistance to it is not a matter of court cases and county legalities. It is hard, bloody, and warlike. The delays set up by the "all deliberate speed" absurdity allowed the Klan to revive itself massively as a direct action and terror group.

When the regenerated NAACP branch, under the leadership of Williams and another remarkable young leader, Doctor Albert Perry, began to press for desegregation, or, in the swimming pool matter, for some elementary justice and humanity, the Klan began its classic role of terror. Cars have replaced horses, but the tactics are as childish as ever. Hooded men in white robes, purchased from the Klan's official supplier, a famous mail-order house in St. Louis, sitting in cars with the dome lights on, with engines racing and horns blowing, rode through the streets of Newtown, shooting into the windows of homes, grills, barber shops, poolrooms, and stores.

This had always worked before; for a hundred years men with guns and the right to use them at will had lorded it over people without them and no rights at all. The Klan rode in Monroe, North Carolina, in 1867, and by its incessant and officially winked-at brutality, had been able to reverse the agony and blood of the victory at Appomattox and put a whole people back into a bondage, by terror and abuse, even more humiliating than the legal one . . . the one the Emancipation Proclamation was supposed to erase. A public policy of violent threat followed by violent action had worked in Nazi Germany; it is working now in South Africa. For those who want separation of the races, there has never been a better tactic.

Because of the supraofficial status of the Klan in Southern life, the laws concerning the carrying and the shooting off of weapons of death are loosely drawn. Williams decided to take advantage of this contradiction. He wrote away to the National Rifle Association in Washington, D.C., for a rifle club charter. He explained that he was a Marine veteran and had organized a group of ex-servicemen committed to the active preservation of their own and their country's freedom. This is true, of course, in every respect. The charter was sent with alacrity as it always is to any group making such a request, and no one would have given it a second thought if it had been a group of Southern white men.

When it became known that Williams had received such a charter, and had already organized and was thus about to legitimately arm a group of black veterans, the white liberals who had supported him as a poet rejected him as a warrior and ran for cover. There were some few notable exceptions to this, and the police harassment these real patriots underwent is nearly incredible. All the prophetical qualities the white liberals recognized in Williams went

whirling over the dam of their own racist fears; they prac-
ticed, unconsciously, the same sort of denial of basic rights
for which they held the White Citizens Council and the
Klan in such contempt.

It was sad for Williams and everyone else involved, I
assume, to come to the end of the pleasant integrated relationships of the Unitarian Fellowship, but the saddest note
struck here is when the fifty or sixty black men of Monroe
who made up the rifle club gazed at the backs of the retreat-
ing white liberals and realized that they did not need them
anymore. Sad for the whites, I mean, everywhere.

It is sad because many white Americans are troubled to
the point of desperation by this tragic separation. Their con-
sciences are badly lacerated by this increasing alienation of
people, one from the other. They realize that while it goes
on, we are all not only half citizens, but half men and half
women, with our affectional qualities shut off from fulfillment with twenty million others by laws contrived and enforced against us all. And some white Americans are troubled
with nightmare fears that the day of total liberation for the
darker peoples of the world, so rapidly approaching, will be
one of reckoning and revenge, and that they will follow our
path in allocating all the fruits of victory according to the
pigmentation of the skin.

Williams' association with the Unitarian Fellowship was
the only redemptive factor which emerged for him when he
returned to Monroe. Their desertion of him was catastrophic.
It appears that these Unitarians only half understood
the historical position of their denomination in respect to
racial tyranny. If Theodore Parker is a Unitarian apostle,
as they claim he is, and if their present faith exists in some
semblance of his prophetical image, as they boast it does,
then they should have known what Parker did under exactly
similar circumstances in his own time, and done likewise.

When Theodore Parker was confronted with a threat to

black members of his congregation by white racists, he did not tell them to go and kneel on the steps of the church and grovel until the hard hearts of their tormentors were softened. First of all, he took them into his home and under his protection. And then:

> I armed myself and put my house into a state of defense. For two weeks I wrote my sermons with a sword in the open drawer under my inkstand and a pistol on the flap of the desk, loaded, ready, with a cap on the nipple. Commissioner Curtis said, "A process is in the hands of the Marshall . . . in the execution of which he *might be called upon to break open dwelling houses and perhaps to take life by quelling resistance, actual or threatened.*" I was ready for him. I knew my rights.

This is among the mildest of his statements. At the Anti-Slavery Convention in 1837, he said:

> I saw it stated in the Newspapers some time since, that during a debate in the Senate, a southerner charged Mr. Wilson with saying, "that the slaves had a right to rise in insurrection and cut their masters' throats," and Mr. Wilson replied that he had never said so. I should not have been sorry to be a Senator from Massachusetts when such a question was asked. I would have called the attention of the Senate, of the South, and of the world, to my words and then replied, that I not only think, but am sure, that the American slaves have the natural, moral right to rise in insurrection and cut their masters' throats for the sake of their freedom and the time may come when it will be their natural, moral duty to do so; and if I were held in bondage as they are, in the center of the continent and a file of men two thousand miles long stood between me and my natural liberty, then I would split that thread of life from end to end and secure my natural right to liberty, even if I hewed down a man at every step and walked blood red from Texas to Canada. It is high time that this was said, at Washington, and at Boston. Why, what means that pile of stone at Bunker

Hill? what the celebration of the great days of the revolution and the memory of its men.

This was in Boston, Massachusetts, and Parker was consciously acting against the law. How much more compelling is the duty of liberal whites to defend their associates in the Carolinas where the harassment of others is patently against the law? They may offer the excuse that conditions were enormously worse then, that it was slavery times and that the upheaval to come made the humanitarian acts of men like Parker, more virtuous, more justifiable.

But what are the present conditions in the South? The best reporter of the New York *Times* has described them, and nobody has really disputed the accuracy of his statements:

> Every channel of communication, every medium of mutual interest, every reasoned approach, every inch of middle ground, has been fragmented by the emotional dynamite of racism, reinforced by the whip, the razor, the gun, the bomb, the knife, the torch, the mob, the police, and many branches of the state's apparatus.

Some people think that because these things are mentioned in the *Times* that it will soon be cleared away. As a people, we are childishly hopeful that exposure and discussion of a social wrong will cure it. Our sympathies are used up and appeased in the reading while the question of how to defend oneself against the reality of these intolerable conditions goes begging. Now we even have to argue whether the Negro has the *right* not alone the duty, to defend himself and his family. Whenever this question is raised, it is inevitably extended to the false premise that to give these people means of defense is to incite them to run amok and kill as promiscuously as white mercenaries kill Congolese.

The Klan publicly announced and held a monstrous rally with the fires, the crosses, the robes, the booze. Several thousand racists were whipped into a froth of destructive hate by a Baptist preacher, who, after the way of his kind in the South, blessed the coming attack in the name of God, Mother, and Flag. At the end, the Benediction, I believe it is called, the Klansmen staggered into their cars, lit the dome lights, revved up the motors, and started down the highway to get Williams and his rifle squad. The doctor, Perry, had built himself one of the finest houses around, a long low, brick structure of fortresslike strength. The house stands upon a knoll and can be plainly seen from a major highway, Route 74. It is a standing rebuke to the ineffectuality of the Klan's headquarters not far off. Since one of the major humiliations of the oppression of the black citizens of the United States is that it is carried out so publicly, so shamelessly, at high noon in the streets, in public restaurants, in public schools, hospitals, and in the public press, everyone in Monroe knew what was going to happen that night.

The Monroe Chapter of the National Rifle Association were at Doctor Perry's. They erected sandbag emplacements at various shielded and strategic points around the Perry house. They had closed off, with a huge naval chain, one of the entrances of the road passing it. When the long, lethal, cacophonous caravan drew near with its load of destruction and woe, the rifle club, returning the Klan shouts, caught the invaders in a rain of enfilading fire. The first car was decisively hit. There was the harsh sound of breaking glass, an abrupt silence, and then the agonizing grind of dozens of cars going into reverse and groaning backward like some terminal prehistoric animals in the death throes which would bring their whole species into oblivion. No one knows yet what happened to the car zeroed in on that night. The incident was perfunctorily reported in the local press and mentioned in *Jet* magazine, but it never got on the national wire service ticker tapes, the rifle squad organized by Robert Williams had stopped the Klan in its tracks. The city fathers actually outlawed Klan motorcades through the town, whereas before they had been escorted by police cars. It would seem that this tactic would have been widely praised and copied in other centers of Klan terror and control. But actually, it was suppressed as news. The *enemy*, the white racist Americans who were their neighbors, with whom they lived out their lives in constant proximity, whom they worked for, whose government they supported with their toil and their taxes, and their lives on foreign fields of battle, turned to other forms of harassment, legal and economic, against the Negro people of Monroe, North Carolina.

In 1960, when the outbreak of student demonstrations against segregation rose to a climax, some students of Johnson C. Smith College in Charlotte, North Carolina, asked Williams to lead them in sitting-in at Jones' Drug Store in Monroe. Nine students and Williams occupied stools there, instead of standing up in the back, the accepted position of the Negro customer. No threats of violence were used or charged. The proprietor refused service; they sat about fifteen minutes and then walked out. As Williams stood on a nearby street corner, discussing further action, he was arrested on a charge of criminal trespass. Convicted in the trial court, he then appealed to the Superior Court which confirmed the sentence. Williams then sought a reversal in the Supreme Court of North Carolina. His argument was that police enforcement of the trespass statute constituted state action depriving the appellant of the equal protection of the law under the Fourteenth Amendment. This was rejected by the North Carolina Supreme Court, but Williams won his argument in the U.S. Supreme Court.

In Williams' view, the Monroe sit-in was an important example to the desegregation struggle. In an interview in Chicago in February, 1961, he pointed out that "There was less violence in the Monroe sit-in than any other sit-in in the United States. This is because we showed the willingness to defend ourselves. We didn't appear on the streets of Monroe as beggars depending on the charity and generosity of the white supremacists. We appeared as people with strength. And it was to the mutual advantage of all parties concerned that peaceful relations be maintained. For that reason we had less violence. But this is the sort of thing that the supporters of nonviolence never tell. In other communities there were Negroes who had their skulls fractured. But not a single impolite word was passed in Monroe. This means that we've had less violence because we've shown the willingness and the readiness to fight: because of this fact, we've not had to fight; there's been no cause to fight. And we believe that this is a deterrent against violence."

Williams went one day to the local court for a clear look at legal procedures and processes from the standpoint of the black man. He saw, in stately sequence, all the essential fraudulence of the legal process when it has no objectivity, and is, therefore, not just . . . when the courts are used to palliate, to explain away crime, leaving social situations which should be unbearable untouched, because the brute facts are never met head on.

He saw a white man escaping a Grand Jury indictment in the face of the brute fact that this man had kicked a Negro chambermaid down four flights of stairs because she had made a clatter with her wash pail when he was trying to sleep . . . kicked and cuffed her down the stairs and across the landings so roughly that she had to remain in the hospital several months. He saw an epileptic black man given two to five years for attempted rape for touching the wrist of a white woman during an argument over a tractor. He heard a white woman testify that she saw a white man come into a cornfield drunk and attempt to rape a black woman eight months pregnant, in her presence. Williams heard the white jury acquit the assaulter almost without stirring in their seats. He saw, transpiring before his eyes, acts of atrocity which in

other lands, other times, and even in this land, move men to
the breaking point.

And he emerged from this demonstration at his breaking point, filled with the bile and wrath of the outraged
prophet. What could his rifle club do about this profound
injustice? Absolutely nothing! They could not storm the
courthouse and cry out for equal justice under the law, or for
the removal of false judges, as our founding fathers did in
Massachusetts before and after the Revolution. Only white
racists can storm courthouses and jails with impunity and
then only if it is to drag out helpless blacks and shoot them, as
they did Mack Parker in Mississippi.

The hopelessness of the black man's segregation from justice iteslf was so overwhelmingly clear to Williams that when
a wire service reporter approached him, warily, but occupa-
tionally, for Williams is a marvelous agitator and comes up
with newsworthy quotes on all occasions, and asked him what
he thought of the session, Williams replied with words of
fire and doom: "This court has proved that Negroes cannot
receive justice from the courts. They must convict their
attackers on the spot. They must meet violence with violence."

This statement was widely scattered on the news wires,
and Williams was immediately proclaimed as an advocate of
the same sort of mindless cruelty as the Southern whites: the
taking up of arms in a spirit of irrational, indiscriminating
brute force.

Once Williams had been successfully smeared as the
advocate of vindictive violence, the front pages and the TV
screens resumed their favorite visible image of the desegregation movement . . . black men on their knees praying for
mercy, black women being hauled off to prison soulfully
singing of their undiminished love for their oppressors, blacks
unresisting, being thrown through the air like bundles of

rags by white thugs while the local police stand by with complacent smiles. There was some news of Williams, but it was all bad — for him and for his people. Those who nobly dared to be free were forgotten. The national NAACP suspended Williams for his statement.

In the words of a trained social worker highly conversant with the situation at that time, "The Negroes in Monroe need help of all kinds very badly. The state government pretends the situation does not exist. Groups such as CORE, NAACP, and the SCLC, are staying away because they feel that the reputation for violence in that area may hurt their cause. The Negro community is under excessive pressure even for a Southern rural town. Health and welfare services are withheld in ratio to the defiance of the individual to the approved 'status' of the Negro as determined by the white in-group. Robert Williams was the militant Negro there and the white community seemed to go to any length to silence him. He did keep arms in his house and publicly announced this. He told me, and I believed him, that he did this in order to prevent attack upon his family and household by the whites. I believe he would have been killed if the white community in Monroe had not been afraid of Williams' arms."

This virtual obliteration of the black people of Monroe from the thoughts and sympathies of the liberal whites who were pouring money into those areas of the South where the struggle was purely nonviolent and prayerful must have bothered Williams. He must have blamed himself for this neglect. And so a demonstration based on nonviolent techniques was tried at the segregated swimming pool. It was not effective and ground was lost. The Klan brought out their guns again and fired over the heads of the nonresistants. Then the local agent for General Motors tried to ram Williams' small car off the road. The police saw this; Williams demanded the agent's arrest for assault with intent to kill, but the police only laughed. Williams sent in a report of this incident, as he did on all such infractions of the law, to the responsible North Carolina officials and the Federal Department of Justice. Nothing happened . . . nothing was changed.

This grinding attrition, this forced suspension of the basic human impulse to fight back was becoming unbearable to everyone. A group of Freedom Riders decided to give Monroe a helping hand. With their training and their advanced social techniques, it was thought that they could focus some cleansing light, some publicity on the stifled Monroe situation. And so they came, and so the old white violence started up again in Courthouse Square. And Williams and the rifle squad, who had not relinquished their own convictions of self-defense, found themselves, that Sunday night of August 1, 1957, back where they had been when first they raised their guns and fired back at the Klan.

Williams had been opposed to this demonstration. He had been able to live for six years in the racist heartland and been able to walk the streets, engage in protest, and present plans for the alleviation of his people's wrongs in an atmosphere of comparative respect and attention. But the white liberals, who had the money he needed, kept bearing down on him to accept the popular version of the liberation struggle, the one that got all the headlines. They began putting strings on all the answers to his appeals. And even though he had the Klan at a standoff, there were black children in his town growing up without education, without shoes, without food . . . old people without medical attention and minimum comforts. But, he said:

> from all the money raised in the North, no one will send
> a penny to North Carolina, because the white liberals who
> raised this money consider us outlaws and thugs. They
> would rather let us suffer than identify themselves with our

stand. These liberals raised thousands of dollars, they send truck convoys of food and clothing everywhere else in the South, yet they penalize us because we took a militant stand.

Williams felt perhaps it was wrong for him to deny others any relief because of his own principles so he reluctantly gave the word and seventeen Freedom Riders, black and white, and some young lads from Williams' neighborhood began hitting the line around the Union County Courthouse for six days. The experienced pickets walked softly and carried signs that met the specifications of the local police ordinances. They had just come from forty-five horrible days and nights in the Jackson, Mississippi, jails and they knew what awaited them here. They had been beaten in Mississippi jails, Texas jails, Alabama jails; the innocent white boys, the desperate black boys, coming down from the North to show on their vulnerable young bodies the awful stigmata of racist wrongs which lie under the skin of all Americans. They wanted this stigmata to appear on their own bodies in hope that their bruised human flesh would finally get all of us to do something about this deep human shame.

But all they really did was to spread deep into South Carolina — the border is scarcely ten miles away — the news that nonviolent, un-self-defending civil-rights workers were making trouble in Monroe. During the six days, the mob of drunken white racists built up to over five thousand. They stood around the pickets while their shouted threats and obscenities became faster and more constant, like the top of a pot of oatmeal coming to a boil . . . a hate both feeding and consuming these citizens of the United States. The angry, broken murmur of curses and threats at the end of the sixth day, rose to a chant. The area of explosion spread like a flowing pool of gasoline creeping to a source of ignition.

Then the picket line broke up. A white girl got into a car with a black man. A strapping racist harridan lunged at her, tearing at her dress to rip it off and expose her to shame

. . . another spat in her face . . . a small, venomous man,
the local head of the Klan, shrieked out his abysmal horror
at the white girl sitting with the "nigger." Then the mob let
go, beating down the pickets, while the police began to run
them off to jail. Some of Williams' men, armed, began to come
to the borders of the white town, firing guns. A short battle
broke out, long enough for some of the pickets to escape into
the ghetto.

Williams was caught in a tragic dilemma. The pacifist
position of the Freedom Riders had allowed a huge buildup
in the town against him. He was completely outnumbered; he
had lost the initiative. He believed that "when an oppressed
people show a willingness to fight in formidable forces, the
enemy, who is a moral weakling and a coward, is more willing to grant concessions and work for a respectable com-
promise. Psychologically, we must also consider that the
racist whites think themselves superior beings; therefore, they
are not willing to exchange their superior lives for inferior
ones. They are most vicious and violent when they can
practice violence with impunity."

He felt that the mob, fortified by the police, their ap-
petites whetted by the bloody episode in the square, would
ride in a motor caravan into the ghetto, shooting and raping
in the same old sick way. Williams believes that one hundred
years of permissive hatred and violence against the blacks has
made most Southern whites absolutely impervious to the pain
they bring to others, and that there is no atrocious act in the
whole human record of torture and affront beyond their capabilities. He had his rifle squad and all the armed blacks he
could muster . . . only a little over a hundred, standing in
the street, watching the sun, hanging like a time bomb on the
edge of the horizon. He knew, or he felt, that when it
dropped, the Klan would ride. No wonder it was an American black man who wrote one of the most beautiful of the
world's laments: "I hate to see the evenin' sun go down."

But then the event turned into a tragicomedy. Two white clowns, a man and wife, "sight-seeing" the violence, came driving into the ghetto. They were seized, and a chaotic, futile attempt was made to use them as hostages to get the Freedom Riders out of jail. The rumor spread, countrywide, that insanely ferocious blacks had kidnaped a white couple and were torturing them to death. In no time at all it reached the office of the Attorney General himself, Robert Kennedy, who said, "On the basis of the facts reported to me, I would hope the persons responsible for the violence, including the holding of a man and his wife as hostages, will be prosecuted to the full extent of the law."

Now it was a "kidnaping case." Small police planes began circling over the ghetto. State police, local police, deputized residents, were massed around the ghetto, ready to shoot their way in even if it meant extermination of all the residents. Williams and his rifle squad had a brief meeting to decide whether to continue their resistance and to die under the massed white fire of the state. In the meantime, the white couple was returned to their side, completely unharmed. Willams took no part in the discussion. It was decided, by a vote, that the odds were really too much; the delicate balance of force against force that had worked for years was hopelessly flawed. Williams was told to leave, with his family, and "tell their story." He did.

The wisdom of this decision was quickly proven by an FBI "Wanted" circular, where he is described in the jargon used for a carful of drunken, homicidal bank robbers, careening down a road with tommy guns blazing out of every window. He was explosively referred to as "heavily armed" and "extremely dangerous" and as a "schizophrenic." This poster, which hung for nearly a year in post offices all over the country, seemed like an open invitation for trigger-happy police to shoot first and ask questions after. If he had stayed, he would have been put into the custody of a police chief who

had announced, during the trouble, that he would have
Williams "hanging by his heels in the Courthouse Square in
thirty minutes." In the FBI circulars, justifications had to be
offered that he was armed, dangerous, and schizophrenic,
but in Monroe, North Carolina, just being black is enough.

I had known Williams since he stood off the Klan. We
had corresponded and exchanged John Brownisms. It was
then the heyday of Martin Luther King. King's ready access
to almost all national media — which fitted perfectly with the
great liberal doctrine that "as long as you can talk about
something, you can do something about it" — and his passage
in and out of Southern jails, which had become almost a
national sabbatical observance, well illustrated by every form
of picture taking, seemed to make him the true prophet of
the black liberation movement. His prayers and protestations
of love for his enemies, his dignity, the appeal power of his
serious, intact personality, the overwhelming invulnerability
of his moral position seemingly left nothing to be desired in
him but the stamina to last out, in his person, a struggle
which he constantly compared to Gandhi's forty-year effort
to free India.

Williams, on the other hand was either completely ig-
nored or viciously attacked by the press. And after he went to
Cuba he was described in the language hitherto reserved for
Benedict Arnold. I tried very hard, during those years of *We
shall overcome* to interest people in Williams and his self-
defense position, but nobody in the civil-rights movement
wanted to listen. They thought he was "damaging the movement." James Wechsler, the great liberal, was approached at
one point to say a good word for him and the embattled
people of Monroe but he brushed them off, saying "Williams
is a bad guy." It is true that Williams had a bad image, but
history has a curious way of selecting the most unlikely and
unloved people for its charismatic figures. I must confess it

was the sheer "orneriness" of Williams that caught my eye, my attention, and my profound sympathy.

The fact that he was kept out of the press, that he was difficult, that he could not adjust himself to loving his enemies, that he was almost always vituperous and undiplomatic toward the political rulers of the South and had made implacable enemies of them all, from the Governor of North Carolina, who called full-dress press conferences to denounce him, down to the chief and the rest of the police force in his hometown, who called him to tell him he would be hanging in the square before the courthouse in a few minutes . . . this makes me hear in him the thunder from Mount Sinai.

Williams' policy of armed self-defense was both rightful and revolutionary. Most people, including Thoreau, feel they have the right to kill under certain conditions. Nobody feels that this is the statement of a homicidal maniac. It is invoked only under highly exceptional conditions when one human atempts to murder another. Those who take a good look at the Declaration of Independence will find the same doctrine prevailing . . . that the government may be overthrown under certain drastic conditions. These conditions are always obvious. There never has to be a conspiracy to create them, or to act upon them.

Williams' open advocacy of self-defense used to arouse all the antagonisms of an open revolutionary position, but he felt that he was acting within the legal structure of the country. He sent wires and announcements to the press, the Governor, the Attorneys General of the state and nation, the FBI every time he took an action, or received an affront. He was perfectly open about everything. Some guns were shipped in to him from a little Baptist Church and were intercepted and examined by the whites in Monroe, before delivery. A local white newsman called Williams' lawyer in New York, Conrad Lynn, about this, ranting hysterically over the phone

about what they had just "found out." Lynn said, "I thank
you for informing us of their safe arrival."

Williams based his justification on the Fourteenth
Amendment. It says, quite clearly, that

all persons born or naturalized in the United States, and
subject to the jurisdiction thereof, are citizens of the United
States, and of the States wherein they reside. No state shall
make or enforce any law which shall abridge the privileges
and immunities of citizens of the United States, nor shall any
state deprive any person of life, liberty or property, without
due process of the laws, nor deny to any person within
its jurisdiction, the equal protection of the laws.

It is obvious to the feeblest intelligence that this act is
broken every day, every moment in the South. Every racist
law, every exclusion because of color is a violation of it. It is
also obvious that it is revolutionary, that it has the quality of
continuous revolutionary principle in it. The South knows
this and resisted it with every counterrevolutionary tactic at
its disposal. The men who drew this law *made* it revolutionary. The thrust of its enforcement is constantly in head-on
collision with the de facto political structure of the South.
One or the other must go down. It is a law which symbolized
at the time of its passage, and will still more symbolize at the
moment of its full consummation, the working together of
the black and the white to make this a government of the
people. The Abolitionists set it up. The defeat of the Confederacy, and the fears of its resurgence, made this imperative. It was freely admitted that it conferred on Congress "the
power to invade any state to enforce the freedom of the African in war or peace."

Those who now stand agape in horror at the black insurrections should realize that this program to nationalize the
inalienable rights of our citizens, a program adopted twice
by constitutional amendment, once by legislative enactment
over a presidential veto, and again, in 1954, confirmed in its

essence by the full bench of the Supreme Court, has been ruthlessly violated in all parts of the country. Williams implanted in his community the feeling that they were all citizens and men. If the government could not protect their rights by due process, then they must do it themselves. He simply would not recognize that he, because of his color, was barred from any of the privileges and immunities of the whites . . . particularly if those privileges were part and parcel of a governmental structure, paid for by government funds. This conferred on him, so he thought, a legality that superseded the racist legality of Southern municipal law. It made a virtue, an act of patriotism and faith, out of resistance.

When he lived in Monroe he put out a little paper called the *Crusader*. He continued it in Cuba. It now comes out in China. It still sounds as if he had never left home. He has not integrated himself into the revolutionary optimism of these countries. He wakes up in the morning as an American black man who is oppressed. At lunchtime he eats as an American black man who is oppressed. At night he goes to bed as an American black man who is oppressed. I know this, because I saw him in Cuba in 1963 and he talked as if he had never left Monroe, North Carolina!

Lincoln talked once about the mystic chords of memory that link the whites, North and South, together . . . the memory of their old revolution. There are the same kind of mystic chords, hidden continuities linking Williams and the people in the black ghettos. He speaks to them through many organizations . . . some of the most militant black nationalist groups look upon him as their leader in exile. RAM, the Revolutionary Action Movement, makes no bones of the fact that its members were brought together by the concepts of Williams. They feel that they represent a third force somewhere between the Black Muslims and SNCC. Their philosophy is a revolutionary nationalism, for black people only. They feel that the darker races of the world are all enslaved by the same forces, those of white imperialism. They feel that they must take their places in the world of colonial revolutionaries rising against the white taskmasters. To do this, they will follow in the spirit of black revolutionaries like Gabriel Posser, Toussaint L'Ouverture, Denmark Vesey, Nat Turner, Sojourner Truth, Harriet Tubman, Frederick Douglass, Marcus Garvey, W. E. B. Du Bois, and Robert Williams to create a world free of colonialism, racism, imperialism, exploitation, and national oppression.

Robert Williams, quoted on back of RAM's publicly and widely circulated manifesto, says:

> We prefer peaceful negotiations, but our oppressors have proved to us that they are not susceptible to such mild pressures for reform and that they will utilize massive violence to attempt to contain our struggle. When massive violence comes, the USA will become a bedlam of confusion and chaos. The factory workers will be afraid to venture out on the streets to report to their jobs. The telephone workers and radio workers will be afraid to report. All transportation will grind to a standstill. Stores will be destroyed and looted. Property will be damaged and expensive buildings will be reduced to ashes. Essential pipe lines will be severed and blown up and all manner of sabotage will occur. Violence and terror will spread like a firestorm. A clash will occur inside the armed forces. At U.S. military bases around the world local revolutionaries will side with Afro G.I.'s. Because of the vast area covered by the holocaust, U.S. forces will be spread too thin for effective action. U.S. workers, who are caught on their jobs, will try to return home to protect their families. Trucks and trains will not move the necessary supplies to the big urban centers. The economy will fall into a state of chaos.

Robert Williams believed, just as John Brown believed, that he could attack the government with force and arms while professing to be a loyal member of it, operating within its framework. Brown rationalized this at first in a letter he sent to Frederick Douglass in 1854:

> Dear Sir, I have thought much of late of the extreme wickedness of persons who use their influence to bring law and order and good government and courts of justice in disrespect and contempt of mankind . . . among the first are men who, neglecting honorable and useful labor to seek office and electioneer, have come to be a majority in our national legislatures, and who there pass unjust and wicked enactments, and call them laws.

Here, pure and strong, comes the old cry of the Puritan that a law his conscience cannot assent to is no law at all, the cry that came up from the town meetings and the training fields of New England, back in 1774. It convinced John Adams that the Revolution existed and was already won in the hearts and the minds of the people. Good government, to Brown and Adams, and to Robert Williams, was a just government and laws, and officers of law who act differently toward black people than they do to whites reveal that a tyranny exists within the law that needs resistance and correction.

6.

NO MORE LESSER EVIL FOR ME

OUR great fear of revolution in this country comes not from its lawlessness but because it is lawful, and built into the stone and mortar of the foundation. This is why we have to keep the black man or any oppressed minority from taking up arms at all costs. This is why we insult the black people by appointing their leaders for them, and go on to injure them by destroying their real leaders, men like Epton and Williams, like Malcolm.

We offer in their place men like Bayard Rustin, whose deepest concern during the massacres of his people was that "good leaders, nondestructive leaders must be maintained at all cost." It was this same fear of revolution which dictated the nature of the civil-rights struggle, wherein more warriors than at any other time in history went forth to battle with advance notice to the enemy that they would fall before they would fight.

It was Bayard Rustin who cried out, at the height of the murderous gunfire into ghetto homes, that the rioting must be stopped, and "whatever force necessary must be used." What did he mean by this? That the rioters should be shot dead in their tracks, that snipers should be betrayed and executed on the spot by the black people themselves. He was giving a green light to white mercenaries to shoot down his own people.

The relationship of men like Rustin, Roy Wilkins, and Whitney Young to the black rebellions stunningly reveals the extent of their leadership. The black people acted as if they never existed. This was one of the most significant things about the upheavals. When this "Negro leadership" says, . . . "there is no injustice that justifies the present destruction," they are putting plate-glass windows, television sets, six-packs of beer — *things* that can be bought and sold by anyone with a few dollars in their pockets — on an equality with the long, unrelieved, and deadly agony of the black people. This is monstrous.

Their voice is not only that of the white exploiter who cannot bear to see his things destroyed; it echoes the fears of the white liberal. Rustin said, "There will be a fantastic backlash from white people who are weary and frightened of the Negro."

That is correct, but how do you make them unweary and unfrightened? Mass suicide is the only answer to that one. If he expects the black people to live out their lives so that they will not weary and not frighten the whites, then the only solution is the gas chamber. All the whites have to do is get off his people's back, and then both races will be unweary and unfrightened!

"There will be a fantastic backlash in Congress," Rustin says. This is another irrelevancy. He acts as if Congress was a place where the black man, and the white man as well, is tolerated only on condition of good behavior, or its version of it. Congress is supposed to be *us,* the people, all the people. There is nothing sacred about it as a body. When it is not for us, then *it* has to go, not us! And here clearly is the voice of the white liberal . . . "If the riots continue, they will be a threat to all civil liberties. Unconstitutional laws of repression may be passed."

So the white man is saying, "Cool it, black man, or they will get on our backs. We will lose our edge, our God-given, constitutional right to loot, starve, and beat you, under the law. We will be repressed and it's all your fault . . . because we had *freedom, justice, and equality* before you made this irresponsible demand for what we've got. Now we will be shut up into ghettos with the rats and the high rents and the rotting stinking walls and the filth to grow on. So don't rock the boat."

White liberals were always like this. When John Brown rocked the boat at Harper's Ferry with a combined guerrilla force of black and white kids not much older than the black revolutionary lads of today, Horace Greeley, a good man in his way, as the four Negro leaders are good men in their way, said it was all wrong for the old man to do this with violence . . . it could all be accomplished "by the quiet diffusion of the sentiments of humanity without any outbreak." So they were against rocking the boat then, in 1859. And a white revolutionary, Henry D. Thoreau, saw through this, as we must:

> The slave ship is on her way crowded with its dying victims; new cargoes are being added in mid ocean; a small crew of slaveholders, countenanced by a large body of passengers, is smothering four millions under the hatches, and yet the politician asserts that the only proper way by which deliverance is to be obtained is by "the quiet diffusion of the sentiments of humanity without any outbreak." As if the sentiments of humanity were ever found unaccompanied by its deeds, and you could disperse them all finished to order, the pure article, as easily as water with a watering pot, and so lay the dust. What is that I hear cast overboard? The bodies of the dead that have found deliverance. This is the way we are "diffusing" humanity and its sentiments with it.

The sound we hear today of something cast overboard is the dropping by the black people of what the New York

Times, NBC, CBS, and all other white organs of communication call the "Four National Negro Leaders." And they
know it, as Rustin puts it. "If the rioting continues, an atmosphere will be created in which the established civil rights
leadership will be robbed of standing." What does he mean
by *standing?* In whose eyes? He clearly means standing in the
white man's opinion. Then he says, "The movement could be
destroyed and the leadership passed over to the hands of
destructive elements in the ghetto."

The destructive elements in the ghetto are trying to
destroy the ghetto and the forces which preserve it. It is hard
to see what is wrong with this mode of destruction. He seems
unable to realize that what is happening, this telling-revolu-
tion, also has a message for him and his kind . . . that he has
been fired from his leadership as incompetent and irrelevant
. . . that the broken glass and litter in the streets are the bitter
fruits of all his years of "negotiating" and "dialogue" with
the white power structure.

And if the white man has to lose his civil liberties by
general and congressional repressive acts brought on by
these black insurrections and he has to "live like the niggers,"
then he can start singing, "We shall overcome someday,"
about himself, and his wife and his children. He will learn a
lot from this. How the shoe fits. And because he is one
hundred eighty million instead of twenty, he will probably
omit the "someday." He won't even have to go up against the
cops. He can fire them. He can stop making the bullets, the
guns, the tear gas, oxgoads, jeeps, and tanks, paying the taxes
that in turn keep the fat cats in Congress that are going to
"repress" him. He may not have enough sense or enough guts
to do this. But he will want to do it, his built-in instincts, his
consciousness will urge him to do it. He'll want to break
windows, get a few of the goodies, shoot at a few cops.

The abolitionists knew this, as they knew everything else
about this racist country, and this struggle since 1830, except

how long it was going to take. Garrison knew in 1852 why
"Negro leaders" are called Uncle Toms. He explained this,
very clearly, to Mrs. Stowe:

> We are curious to know whether Mrs. Stowe is a be-
> liever in the duty of non-resistance for the white man,
> under all possible outrage and perils, as well as for the
> black man; whether she is for self-defense on her own part,
> or that of her husband or friends or country, in case of
> malignant assault, or whether she impartially disarms all
> mankind in the name of Christ, be the danger or suffering
> what it may. . . . That all the slaves at the South ought to
> . . . wait for a peaceful deliverance and abstain from all
> insurrectionary movements is everywhere taken for granted,
> because the VICTIMS ARE BLACK. But for those whose
> skin is of a different complexion, the case is materially
> altered. When they are spit upon and buffeted, outraged and
> oppressed . . . talk not of overcoming evil with good — it is
> madness, talk not of peacefully submitting to chains and
> stripes . . . it is base servility! let the blood of the tyrants
> flow? Is there one law of submission and non-resistance for
> the black man and another law of rebellion and conflict for
> the white man?

Obviously there is.

The "Negro leader" white liberal position so clearly
expressed by Rustin goes a long way toward explaining
one of the great historical enigmas of the century: how it is
that the most liberal country in the world is also the most
racist (with the possible exception of South Africa, but even
South Africa is not slaughtering at the boasted rate of 1800
per day the brown men of South Asia). It is another example
of the lesser-evil theory which is at the heart of our political
existence. The lesser-evil theory is what makes this kind of
democracy work. It is obviously a lesser evil to let a minority
suffer denial and deprivation than to risk their being inflicted
on the whole, or the majority.

It is a lesser evil to degenerate the overtly rebellious as criminal elements, and say, as Johnson just did on national television, that the riots were not a part of legitimate civil-rights protests, that they were not the "Fire next time." This way the rebellious can be destroyed without honor, and without history. To call them revolutionaries would bring into peril all those who have publicly sympathized with their position and the unspeakable conditions which have brought them into this state of revolt. To call them criminals now cleans the skirts of those who sympathized with them before they committed irrevocable, revolutionary acts.

It is absolutely imperative in a liberal democracy, this lesser-evil theory. Otherwise, how can you live hundreds of years with racism if it is not explained away as a lesser evil than total fascism? Hitler was elected as a lesser evil. So was Johnson. Years ago Brooks Adams, feeling the revolution that he considered a personal inheritance from his grandfather and great-grandfather turning sour in his blood, tried to explain it as the Degradation of the Democratic Dogma: "That it is possible by education to stimulate the selfish instincts of competition, which demands that each man should strive to better himself at the cost of his neighbor, so as to coincide with the common good. . . ." So we have more people in institutions of higher education than ever before; there is more reading, more listening, more "informational" communication than ever before. It is a time when "liberalism" in government and in labor relations is in the ascendancy. Economically we have never been more affluent. We have never "bettered ourselves" more than now. Nor has it ever been more at the cost of our neighbor. Men in labor unions, once the repository in this country of the virtue and highest idealism of man who works and makes things, now bend every muscle to accelerate the killing in Vietnam, and to "better themselves." Boys sacrifice themselves on the battle-fields of the Delta under the illusion that they are working

for the common good of the people of Vietnam. Our dogma
is that self-interest creates a common good . . . and those
whose self-interest does not pay off, who live in filth, unskill,
and unemployment, they must be thrown to the lions as an
obvious lesser evil. Better them than us. Self-interest ignited
the guns of Newark, the fires of Detroit. White self-interest
dictated the nonviolent tactics of the civil-rights struggle
where demonstrating blacks were supported in breaking
specifically racist laws so long as they did not hit back at
policemen and thus threaten the "common good" of "law
and order."

The same people who tell the blacks that this society
murders them, starves them, and keeps them in ignorance
administered these bitter truths with the tranquilizer of nonviolence effectively coating them over. From the late 1950's,
when the black people began showing signs of mounting a
bloody resistance to this tyranny, the leadership of their own
"liberation," from center to left, rolled over them like a
stifling fog, discrediting their leaders, obscuring the immediate crises which made them conscious of an oppression which
had to be fought, decrying their militancy as black racism
and violence, and managing to put off some accursed question crying out for an answer in favor of a "study" that would
lead to a "peaceful and responsible solution in the near
future." The liberals felt, subconsciously, that the seedtime of
real revolt was becoming diluted and washed away in a flood
of wordage and promise, so that one could no longer see the
way things were. The solution became the watery one of pious ideology, pious sociology, pious government money, pious
goodwill and good intentions. The President of the United
States, the day after a black rebellion in the fifth major city
of the United States left thirty-seven dead and over $500,-
000,000 in "damage," advised the nation to go to church
next Sunday and pray for reconciliation between the races.
He sounded exactly like those Southerners, after the Civil

War, getting ready to sell back the liberated slaves to a more efficient bondage.

They tried that already in Detroit; they poured millions into panacea projects there. Sociologically speaking, race relations there were supposed to be better than anywhere in the whole country. But it exploded all the same, because the black people no longer want to add to their other deprivations and humiliations that of being forced to have a cause without a rebellion, of being victims denied a self-generated struggle for their freedom.

The blacks discovered, in fact, that the Aesopian language of the white liberals, condemning violence, was really a fear of some kind of revolutionary action. Somehow they transferred the meanings of the word. *Revolution* became a moderate, gradual approach to the problem; *violence* became antirevolutionary futility, preordained disaster. They not only deformed the revolutionaries into criminals and madmen: they debauched the noble term itself.

And yet the white liberal is morbidly fascinated by violence. As much as he is opposed to it as the destroyer of his tranquility and peace of mind, his attention can always be aroused by its use. Brute force, planned violence, he never sees. As Thoreau pointed out, he will never admit that "we preserve the so-called peace of our community by deeds of violence every day. Look at the policeman's billy and handcuffs. Look at the jail! Look at the gallows. Look at the chaplain of the regiment." Look at the Pentagon today — the most monstrous source of violence the world has ever known.

The "Negro leaders" not only are deaf to their own people; they are obviously not tuned in on the voice of America, the new international language. It speaks violence, and its punctuation is the clatter of bullets, the booming of ships' guns, the grinding of tanks, the lethal reverberations from the bombers. This language of violence is our leading contribution to the culture of the world. We do not hear anything else. We export, we give away, we transport more guns than typewriters and ballpoint pens. We have sold $46,000,000,000 worth of arms to other countries in the last seventeen years. Our government bank, the export-import bank funded through the people's money, has contributed 38 percent of its total loans for arms purchases in countries whose main problem militarily is suppressing its own people's desire for liberation. And the governor of New Jersey calls the breaking of a store window "an atrocity."

Our society, and those we control, directly and indirectly, is becoming so intricate, and so restless and disturbed with the human disparity existing in it, that we can only exist at the point of the gun. Violence has become the shorthand of our method of control. It saves us from typing up the papers, the documents, with which we used to justify some egregious violation of human law. We think the need for violence is always self-evident, and we use it instantly. It is the way we tell what we want, what we value, and what we are going to retain, regardless of the human cost. The sound of breaking glass and tinkling windows merely shows that the black man is learning our language and is now ready to be heard.

Sitting before the television set during the July rebellions, I was filled with an almost Dostoevskian polarity of exultation and fear. It was like being in the eye of the great storm that is passing over this country, sweeping away, with hurricane strength, old assumptions and stabilities, shattering notions and tolerances of all sorts. Eighty black insurrections in a week! People in the ghettos, half starved, half tortured by the circumstances of their daily life; tortured most of all by the affluence and purchasable joy all around them, from which they seem forever shut off, are standing off tanks and men sent up against them in army mobilization and strength. This could not be foreseen by anyone. It has the quality of a myth. It is completely unplanned, leaderless. Emerson would have understood it more than any other American, perhaps, in all its revolutionary vagueness; its formlessness. "Massachusetts, in its heroic day," he said, "had no government — was an anarchy."

And the black revolution is going on so fast, so remorselessly; there is so much action, proliferation that the whole punitive part of our country is off balance. They don't know what to do. They stab at it, and it speeds away to erupt somewhere else. But it has to stop, and then what? I am full of fear of what my people will do to these fighters who nobly dare to be free . . . the whole black people who are daring in such a way. It is too awful to think about the capabilities for punishment we whites can evoke in a moment like this.

These black rebellions are beginning to wedge themselves between the armor plate of political and economic repression in this country in such a way that to dislodge them, the whole structure of repression may have to be dismantled. But we are not a people with the patience, the humanity to do this piece by piece so that the wrong can be extracted in a humane way. The black people, with their pitiful smallness of numbers and their vulnerability, are now wondering what we are going to do to them for nobly daring to be free.

They are thinking of our capacity, even our tendency, for genocide. They know we are capable of considering it a lesser evil. They remember the bomb of one of our liberal Presidents dropped on Hiroshima on August 6, 1945, from a bright blue sky at 8:15 in the morning. There was a blinding flash; the fireball dropped to the ground. A wind blew furiously through the streets of the city. It was a wind that could be seen, a wind of solid flame, dense enough to liquefy the stones of its channel.

Everyone it touched died instantly, but people a mile away felt their skins peel off and hang down like strips of cloth. This happened in utter darkness. Thirty minutes later it got light again, and there was a heavy rainfall of black water which was deadly poison. There were other phases of torture. A whirlwind came up at one o'clock, separating what was left of the half-liquefied buildings and hurling the fragments around like projectiles.

Some 200,000 people were killed in a matter of minutes, and the President was sent an enthusiastic cable saying, "Operated on this morning, stop, diagnosis not yet complete but results exceed expectations, stop . . . interest extends great distance." Three days later, on August 9, 1945, the President of the United States ordered another bomb dropped, this time on Nagasaki.

It exploded just above Uragami Cathedral. The results did not "exceed" but were, perhaps, equal to the "expectations." There was now a predictable pattern; first, tremendous heat, about 50,000,000 degrees centigrade. Then this cooled slightly, and the blast came which blew the people who had not been burned into extinction and which was mingled with the destruction of all the buildings at the hypercenter of the explosion. About 100,000 people were killed at once, but another 200,000 of Hiroshima and Nagasaki people have been dying slowly and painfully for the last twenty-two years.

Here then are two primitive bombs which killed 300,000 people rather quickly and kept another 200,000 in a lifelong concentration camp in which the daily tortures of pain and nausea are inflicted upon them without the necessity of guards, dogs, torture chambers, planned starvation, or uncounted miles of rusting barbed wire.

In the attempt by the insane Nazi racists to solve "the Jewish problem," 6,000,000 innocents were killed. This same 6,000,000 could today be obliterated by just one nuclear bomb, within the span of a single sunny morning. And everybody knows there are now enough bombs in stockpiles to kill everyone on earth as much as ten times over, to effect,

in a day, perhaps, the final solution to the human problem
. . . life.

We know this in America; we know that we are poten-
tial genocides. We have wept long and constantly for the
victims of Buchenwald and the other camps; we still keep
the scar of this in our hearts. No one has forgiven the hands
and brains which gave the orders for the death-camp processes. We call them savages, mindless, and so they were . . .
some sort of unbelievable human regression into the worst
forms of animality.

But what of this stock of bombs we are making and
storing in overkill proportions, with their infinite capacity
to turn the whole world into a solid, flame-filled concentration of fire to liquefy humanity until it deliquesces into
nothingness. Or perhaps it will turn man into some form
of obscene fossil, fused together with inanimate forms of his
culture into a new strata of residual rock which will forever
remain the evidence of man's inadequate moral constitution.

We do not think of ourselves as genocidal, but these
bombs are not made by regressive savages, but by the steady,
deliberate, and difficult toil of the finest and most advanced
minds of our time. By the heirs of the human learning
process since the beginning of man's knowledge about the
universe and his own human condition. Now these super-
minds have made people-extinction the end and purpose of
all their scholarly devotion.

We do not think of ourselves as genocidal, and we have
relinquished all our controls over these weapons and given
our military responsibility for them. And it is true that the
responsibility for the bombs circling the world today, at the
ready, and in the bays of bombing planes, and circling the
seas in iron monsters capable of jetting forth the mushroom
cloud of death, lies directly with our military leaders. But
they too are only men like us — a few button-pushing officers
and bomber pilots. And we have given them life and death

power over the world, trusting to their frail human consciousness . . . a fallible apparatus which can be thrown
out of kilter by a bad meal or a domestic quarrel. The blacks
know more than we do how short the tempers of white men
can be . . . and how easily they can be affected by anger
at people of another color who are "pushing." Johnson
called the Japanese "little yellow dwarfs with knives in their
hands."

The bomb is the instant genocide, the instant Buchenwald which kept the world in a concentration camp of fear
for many years. But we have also a history of exacting a slow,
dragging genocide of the original owners of this land. In
1838 the Cherokee Indians were forced to give up their
lands, towns, and farms in Georgia and travel to a point beyond Missouri. They had been the most "civilized" of all
the Indians, with farms, stores, legislatures, leaders, and
policies equal to, if not in advance of, our own. But the
whites wanted the land and the improvements made on it,
and they would not stop killing, burning them out, raping,
and looting. The United States government, under the great
democratic President Andrew Jackson, dispossessed them,
breaking solemn treaties and agreements. There were 17,000
of them to be driven out. Troops were assembled in such
great numbers as to prevent any show of resistance by the
Indians.

The troops drove families from their dinners and beds
at the point of bayonets down weary miles of trails to filthy
stockades built to confine them until the thousands were
mobilized for the march. A lawless rabble of whites followed
on the soldiers' heels to loot and pillage and drive off the
cattle and stock of the Indians before their feet were off their
own farms. These men hunted through the Indian graves
robbing the jewelry of the dead. Occupants were surrounded
in their houses without warning, children were separated
from their families, husbands from wives.

Within a few days the 17,000 were crowded into stockades. Hundreds sickened and died. Then the procession
began; the sick, the old, children, marching on foot. Every
day they died by the tens and twenties. They left in October,
and it soon got to be winter, and they had nothing to protect
them from the weather. Rivers were running with ice. Sections of the march had to wait in the icy blasts for days,
penned up in wagons or stretched on the ground with a
single blanket to keep out the cold, until the river ran clear
and they could cross. Those at the head of the line killed
all the game. The others starved. Old women with their
lives' possessions, the possessions of their whole families
struggled over the frozen ground with bare feet, slogging
out a ten-mile day. And they were so religious, so Christian-
ized, they would not travel on a Sunday. They finally reached
their destination on the bleak plain beyond Arkansas in
January, 1839. Four thousand of them had died in the removal, either in the stockades or on the march. Then came
the removal of the Chickasaws; the Seminoles, the Creeks
had to go through this. This was followed, year after year
across the whole country . . . all were dispossessed, slaugh-
tered, starved, betrayed, broken: the Cheyenne, the Sioux,
the plains Indians of every tribe . . . they all went down to
genocide at our hands. It was government policy; no one
was punished for this; nobody yet has paid the bill.

Can a nation really atone for this? Can a nation deny
that it is racist, or founded on racism, when these brute facts
loom up in its history?

We are still doing it . . . *today* we are doing it . . .
knowing we are doing it, and looking on the misery of its
victims with as little compassion as the whites in the days of
the Indian removals. There was a story in the back pages of
the Boston *Globe* on June 22. The headline was "Starvation
No Stranger Here." It was about the discovery by a team of
doctors that thousands of our citizens living in Mississippi

were being systematically starved to death and that there was already so much damage done to them physically that they may never be able to live in a normal way, to carry out the functional life of an average person.

The most ghastly aspect of this situation is that it is not an accident at all but represents a calculated if unspoken policy. The Negro poor are no longer an economic asset, because mechanization has largely replaced their cheap labor. Besides, they represent pockets of discontent, threatening the white power structure, as even the most indolent become aware of their civil rights. So drive them north or let them wither to death . . . a kind of genocide on a county scale. The investigating doctors themselves could apparently discover no other explanation for the conditions they found. They saw children for whom hunger is a daily fact of life . . . sickness in many forms an inevitability. We do not want to quibble over words but malnutrition is not what we found, boys and girls we saw were hungry, weak, in pain, sick, their lives being shortened . . . they are, in fact visibly and predictably, losing their health, their energy, their spirits, they are suffering from hunger and disease, directly or indirectly they are dying from them, which is exactly what starvation means.

These doctors were from Harvard, M.I.T. One doctor was from Yazoo City, Mississippi, one from North Carolina. No question that this is not an exaggeration, a communist plot.

The issue at hand is the medical, social and psychological failure of literally penniless rural families. These families are denied medical care, adequate sanitation, welfare or relief payments of any kind . . . unemployment compensation, protection of the minimum wage law, coverage under social security and even recourse to the various food programs administered by the federal and local government. In sum, by many thousands they live outside of every legal, medical and social advance our nation has made.

They are talking there about Mississippi. But it is universal. It is in Roxbury; it is in all the ghettos of the great cities.

We are using human death as an instrument of policy. Genocide has become so familiar and acceptable to us that we have accepted it as normal. We are now engaged in a war in which our progress, our victories are counted only in genocidal terms. I never heard of this before. Wars used to be reported in terms of what armies had surrendered, what fortresses, town, positions taken . . . in the Korean War it was what hill we had conquered and held. Now it is the dead people we count . . . the more the merrier: "Sixty-one Viet Cong were killed today — happily none of our troops suffered casualties." Our progress toward the great society is on the steppingstone of men lying with their life's blood draining into their own blasted and poisoned fields, poisoned by us. We bluntly call our mission there: search and destroy. We have not counted the civilian deaths and those of the children. We have admitted, or one of our old Presidents had admitted, that the people we are killing represent the sentiments and the political desires of the majority of that country's citizens, but we kill on until they will become a living minority, perhaps, but the dead majority will rise in history to resist us and they will forever outvote those who lived to remain under our heels.

What the theory of government is under which these unspeakable acts are being committed is irrelevant. Its practices stand revealed to have been, during the entire longevity of its existence, without justice and without mercy for the whole people of the Indian race, the whole people of the black race, the eternal poor, and the young who are the eternal cannon fodder. The government is their enemy and it must be ours. The system that is grinding them into dust at an accelerating rate, is ours; we are supporting it; it *acts* for us.

Every policeman that whips a black head whips it for us. Every tommy gun, tank, bullet, bull horn, every apparatus brought into the ghetto wars for our usual overkill is paid for by us. Yet we are constantly trying to work out "deals" with the fascists, the racists, the murderers to legislate together, talking constantly of how much civil rights we are going to be able to wrest from this Congress, how much they will spend to "abolish poverty."

Does anybody seriously believe that we can collaborate with the same government that has an Eastland as head of its Justice Committee, and a Stennis as head of its Arms Committee? These men are the Senators from Mississippi, and in the hierarchy of government power, they are responsible for all the Federal Government's relations to their state. And thus they are responsible for genocide, by withholding from sick and starving people the medical care, the welfare and relief funds paid for by our taxes, and by "forcing them to live outside every legal, medical and social advance our nation has made." Thus they are murderers, and instead of collaborating with them, we should be trying and executing them for their murders.

The people who constantly suggest these forms of collaboration are not racist, are not bad people themselves. They are for the idea of revolution, but they cannot even think of violence, of the mess that it will cause. They think the machinery we have, in spite of being cumbersome, will somehow, under the eruptive prodding of the historical process, save us all. They are still talking about getting into the wards, getting into the street, getting into politics, and making the Constitution "work." But even if they did do this, how long would it take to get an Eastland, a Stennis out of power, out of the station from which they do such unspeakable harm to thousands of helpless human beings?

This is the right way to do it, to be sure, peacefully, and constitutionally. Even the revolutionary will admit this.

No revolutionary says he wants people to be offered violence, or to be killed, without justice, without a cruel necessity. The revolutionary is actually a redemptionist. He wants to transform society and make it better. But he knows that the transformation factor in the old revolution was very bad. It made no provisions for the Indian and the slave. We made no plans to convert them to what we were, or wanted to become, or to convert ourselves in some sort of halfway covenant to be like unto them. There was no common wealth, nothing in common. We did not look at them, on a one-to-one basis.

The revolutionary is an optimist. He believes in what he wants, and he thinks other people will. Most people do not believe in what they want . . . they want things of appetite and they hate themselves for it, for getting cluttered up with the waste and the glut it represents. The revolutionary wants to join the millions and have the millions join him. He is a transcendental person and he thinks that in the revolutionary process everyone is going to get transformed and join him.

But once he starts to carry out this process, once he makes a move, the police are on him, various repressive forces act savagely against him, and he has to act back the same way. The great problem in a revolution is not its violence but its terror. Terror long remains in the memory of man. It is another canceling-out factor which people cite to resist real change and carry on for another generation.

But all my life I have been reading the great revolutionary and emancipatory texts of our country. This has formed my consciousness. And I have been sitting in political meetings since I was a boy. And beside me sat a black boy who was supposed to wait for these democratic things to happen. I am fifty-six now. He is fifty-six now. His children are born and they are waiting. His grandchildren are waiting. His father waited and his great-grandfather waited.

I don't have to wait for what they are waiting for. I have it. So I can't pledge their future to my peace of mind. I have to say, "Success to their insurrections, because I have seen how many babies can starve to death, how many brains are damaged, how many bones shriveled while we wait for a nice unmessy peaceful revolution. Every question coming up in the civil-rights struggle could have been solved by the implementation of the Fourteenth Amendment. Every President since 1868 has stood up before the Capitol on Inauguration Day and pledged to uphold this: none of them ever have.

If this Constitution can work, why have so many generations been born, flowered, and died without the good of it? Is the Constitution some kind of a mortgage the black people have to pay off before they can use it? They are saying, We want our freedom now. They have said it with songs, marches, jail sentences, prayers. Now they are saying it with violence. And I have to reply to it not as white Truman Nelson, who bruises easily, and does not get pushed around, but on a one-to-one basis with the nameless, faceless black man who always gets pushed around.

I went through all the customary worship of the democratic structure . . . so beautiful, so attainable if only we can work and wait a little longer. I thought it was too late when I was a boy, but then I discovered people like Theodore Parker and George Ripley and the great abolitionists and I thought if I could only write books and bring back these beautiful old truths and continuities to the people there might be another chance. It is awful to go through all this hope, all this playing with the fig leaf of words that covers our rotting nakedness.

You, and my boy, and my grandfather who was in the Civil War, and my father went to school, and we were all told that this was the land of the brave and the free. And we went to church and they told us that we were our brother's keeper and that we should do unto others as we would have done unto us. This was put into us, into the warp and woof of our existence. Something is blocking us from acting this out. That which is put in us never becomes reality . . . never permeates our life and our conduct toward others. If we can't make it now on what we have been taught, we must find out what is blocking it, what is preventing us from acting it out. It should be there . . . the message should be there . . . why can't we give it?

It has been so long now that I think the only right we have left is the right of revolution. This has been denied us all along. But somewhere in the American consciousness, somewhere among the Sunday School texts and the pictures of the Bunker Hill Monument, there may be . . . there must be a stratum of nonguilt about revolution.

7.

HISTORY IS ON OUR SIDE

HISTORY is on our side, if we know how to use it. Every historian is a revolutionary at heart . . . or should be. He sees every day the long continuity of the wrongs a few people do to the millions under the banners of divine right, national sovereignty, industrial progress, manifest destiny and for the protection of the white race, the master race, a superior culture, or the democratic process. The same people, of course, who commit these wrongs and seize power to achieve them write the history that sanctifies their conquests and makes them impervious to change, short of physical upheaval.

When in the late 1950's the white Southerner was confronted with the validation of the constitutional rights of the black people, he struck back and put down the threat of equality not only with the bomb, the dog, the chain, the prison, the gun, the rope, the tear gas . . . he sanctified his brutality with his history. He opposed black liberation with an organized, band-playing white resistance. It had a country and a flag.

The Confederate flag, the battle emblem of a slave-whipping, slave-degrading, and slave-killing society which went down to deserved defeat a hundred years ago began to appear at the head of hundreds of marches by white Southerners to besiege a school when an attempt to desegregate was being made, to shove aside and spit in the faces of some small, helpless, and vulnerable black children trying to get their education in the regular way. It waved proudly at orgies of moronic white racist students at the few universities trying to desegregate . . . inevitably paired with "Nigger go home" signs and like national obscenities. Long before this it had a tradition of waving over gross offenses against Southern black people at the hands of night riders, lynchers, and burners-alivers. I saw it myself, flying on the antennas of U.S. Army staff cars.

It was invariably coupled with the Stars and Stripes at the ceremonies held not long ago at the centennial of the Civil War. This centennial was the purest expression of white supremacist history and used consciously, I believe, to justify, and even glorify, the South's present resistance to desegregation as an extension, somehow noble, of the glorious "lost cause." There was never the slightest thought given to what the black people would think of it. In fact the mood of North-South "reconciliation" which pervaded it demanded that they be left out.

In all the great public scenes of reenactment, there were no elements of doubt raised that both sides were separately but equally righteous in their cause. The slave and the abolitionist were left completely out, or dismissed in caustic or condescending parenthesis. Lee and Jefferson Davis, along with Lincoln and U. S. Grant were presented as all-American Americans, laboring under a slight and still unresolved Constitutional misunderstanding. The whole titanic drama of millions of black people kidnaped from their homeplace and brought to the land of the free to be used as beasts of burden . . . the burden of guilt they laid then on our hearts: that slaughter then came out of this, and nothing but this; their subsequent days of being liberated, deluded, despised, and thrust back into slavery were never touched upon. For all their agony before the War of Southern Rebellion, no one was found guilty or rebuked . . . no one was presented the bill.

There was a full scale reenactment of the battle of First Manassas, a *Confederate* victory. The interest and ardor of the white South in this spectacle was so intense; the Confederate flag so omnipresent that I remembered what Garrison said about the South, long after Appomattox.

> They are in the Union, but not of the Union. They are under the Constitution but not for the Constitution, except as a matter of duress; they are nominally Americans but really Southerners in feeling and purpose. If they could see their way clear to throw off the authority of the Federal Government and to resuscitate their defunct Confederacy, they would instantly rise again in rebellion and expel every loyal Northerner from their Territorial domain.

The years have proved that they have done this without bothering with the "authority of the Federal Government." Besides, everyone knows of their powerful influence, their dominating influence there. If admirers, followers of the Confederate flag, if Senators, Representatives, bureaucrats, administrators in favor of segregation and of maintaining "the purity of the race" were forbidden to take office or expelled from those they already hold in our government, it would be split asunder, it would be chaos, it would not be able to operate. What would happen if our President, our Secretary of State took this test? Burning the Confederate flag would really smoke them out for what they are. The Secretary of State tells the story that he cannot honestly sign that provision in all security checks that no member of his family has taken arms to overthrow the government because his grandpappy was a Confederate soldier and fought under that flag to destroy the United States government.

The country was treated to a reenactment in Montgomery of Jefferson Davis' taking office as President of the Confederacy. Hundreds of Southern whites in broadcloth and

crinolines took part in this obscenity, celebrating as beautiful and worth remembering a society based on the wild and
tragic fantasy that slavery was right . . . while passing by
them in the streets were the black descendants of the American men and women that this society had fought to keep
enslaved. As usual the resurrected Confederate heroes acted
as if their fellow citizens were not there, as if they were
utterly invisible.

But the black people knew they were there: knew that
these ceremonial rites were the final expiations of the tyranny brought against them while they were slaves. That the
battle soil of the South was now sterilized to the depth of
three generations to remove any suspicions that there was a
racial conflict going on there. They knew that this is how
the white man breaks his continuity of guilt.

The liberal historians' glossing over of slavery is highly
significant. It is kind of an appeal not to mention the guilty
past because it is too shameful to be thought of. They ration-
alize it and excuse it by trying to shift the shame to the black
man himself; they try to make him think of himself as the
helpless victim of slavery (and now "poverty") instead of an
African in chains. They try to make it so that the black man
does not want to talk about, or think about his past in slavery. At the same time they know that unless he does unearth
this experience, and talk about it, he will never succeed in
reconstructing his identity or succeed in understanding racism as a system of tyranny and beginning an attack on it.

But the black men have been probing this past. They
have been reflecting on these hidden continuities. Only they
are placing the guilt where it belongs, on the backs of the
whites. They know that if the historical reprise had been
honestly presented, there would have to be a reenactment of
the Nat Turner insurrection in Virginia, really the first
scene in the war, in which an all-black formation of freedom

fighters carried out the forefathers' injunction that "Resistance to tyranny is obedience to God." Or of the rescue of the fugitive slave Shadrack by Lewis Hayden and other black men from the Boston courthouse, another beginning of the beginning. And it is absolutely unthinkable that the parade of the Fifty-fourth Massachusetts Regiment of black men marching off to kill white racists in South Carolina in 1863, passing the house of Wendell Phillips on Essex Street in Boston, saluting William Lloyd Garrison as he stood there on a balcony with his hand resting on a bust of John Brown, and with the massed bands playing "John Brown's Body" would be reenacted. Or the heroism of any of the 200,000 black soldiers that fought against the racist South . . . of the dying at Fort Pillow, Fort Wagner, and the Crater, where the slain black heroes were thrown into holes like piles of offal and the white officers were thrown in with them . . . "buried with their niggers!"

History is identity. There is no question about this. Look at the people who don't know who they are and who are searching desperately for some kind of personal identification, and you will find they are a people whose history has been taken away from them. Ideology has to do with identity as well, but there is no ideology without history either, because ideology has to come out of the ways things are, and were, and must be; of the usable past, the pragmatic present, and the ascertainable future.

There are many of us who do not know who we are because we are giving our silent consent to injustice and tyranny without knowing of our own continuity of resistance and revolutionary morality. We do not know we should have no consciousness of guilt in putting down that racism pretending to be "law and order." We have taken away not only the whole life of the black people by suppressing their history along with their persons, but we have suppressed, histor-

ically, the lives and works of those whites whose lives have
been inextricably woven into the black resistance movement
of the pre-Civil War period.

Let us take John Quincy Adams, for example, known as
a conservative President, and performing as a conservative
the greater part of his political life. But when his revolutionary conscience became lacerated by American racism, he
had no hesitation in reaching for and proclaiming a revolutionary alternative.

As a boy, Adams saw his father hunted as a traitor by
government soldiers and Tories. He became Jefferson's secretary, a Senator, the Secretary of State, the Professor of
Rhetoric at Harvard; none of the greater glories were denied
him. When he left the Presidency he was expected to settle
grumpily into the role of the elder statesman who has done
his best for his country and sits back, to watch, with malig-
nant satisfaction, the errors and terrors of his successor.

He did not do this. He ran for the House of Representatives and was elected and served there sixteen years. While
he was there he spent most of his time fighting for measures
which aimed at his country's dissolution, or its breaking up
in Civil War. He knew exactly what he was getting into.
"Slavery in the South is a perpetual agony of conscious terror
and guilt attempting to disguise itself under sophistical argu-
mentation and braggart menaces. In the North the people
favor the whites, and fear the blacks of the South." But he
hated, and showed his hatred with his vituperous tongue, the
racism which was increasingly defiling the promise of the
revolution his father had so greatly helped to make.

On January 25, 1842, at the time when it had become
most clear that talking of slavery could split the country
wide open, he took from an untidy pile on his desk a petition
signed by Benjamin Emerson and forty-five other citizens
of Haverhill, Massachusetts. He was now nearly seventy-
four years old. The erosions of time were reminding him

daily — he says "hourly" — of the decay in his body and mind, and creating in him an unquenchable thirst for some repose and relief from his one-sided struggle.

He had fallen in the House and dislocated his right shoulder. The slightest chill would now create a smothering hoarseness to make his speech nearly unintelligible. His hand shook so badly he had to hold one with the other; his eyes so weak and defective that water would trickle constantly down his cheeks. But he was a revolutionary and he found compulsions in his conscience that he could not resist, even though he quailed at the magnitude and danger of the opposition to any attack on slavery.

After his next few words he would be locked in a death struggle with the brute force of men who had the power to whip their servants to death at a refusal or a taunt. At home, the insults and defamations to be heaped upon him would horrify his family, who were already furious because he had exchanged the vested interests of a retired President for the cockpit of a dubious and inglorious struggle.

In twelve days of battle, which increased rather than waned in its intensity, he was able, by the slightest comment, to lash the backs of the slaveholders raw, sending them into such helpless frenzies of rage that they would leave the House in a body under his attacks. The more they attacked him, the more eloquent he grew. It seemed to them that he was inhaling their hostility, their outrage, and their hatred like reviving jets of pure oxygen. He goaded them, day in and day out, on every issue in which the specter of slavery could be raised. There was no one there who could send the young squires of the peculiar institution into a blind fury any quicker, or more economically than he could . . . nor was there any other member who concealed less the gratification that the browbeating of another man could bring him.

Everybody in the country was watching him. "He drinks sulphuric acid in his tea," Emerson said. The debate came about because he was accused of high treason. His defense was the right of revolution. In defending this he was unceasingly insulting, irascible, out of order, ill-tempered, cruelly vituperative, and alone . . . and he was magnificent and he glowed with the incandescence of a prophet who knows that he is right.

The trouble started when he presented the petition from the men in Haverhill. It was to dissolve the Union. The reasons were that there were no longer reciprocal benefits between the sections, that one section was draining the resources of the other without adequate returns, and that if these one-sided actions continued, the nation would be destroyed.

The Southerners thought they had finally trapped Adams . . . that calling on Congress to break its oath to preserve the Union with a proposition to dissolve it was an act of high treason. The following, in which Mr. Adams says *yes* to the right of revolution is taken directly from the record of the debate in the congressional Globe for the second session of the Twenty-seventh Congress of 1842.

Mr. ADAMS: I am not surprised at the charge has been brought against me of high treason. What is high treason? The Constitution defines what high treason is, and it is not for him, or his puny mind, to define what high treason is and confound it with what I have done. Sir, the first volume of the laws of the United States will show what it is. I desire the clerk to read the first paragraph of the Declaration of Independence. (Raising his voice.) The first Paragraph of the Declaration of Independence. (Raising his voice to a still higher pitch.) The first Paragraph of the Declaration of Independence!

The CLERK read as follows:

"We hold these truths to be self-evident, that all men are created equal, that they are endowed by their Creator with certain unalienable Rights, that among these are Life, Liberty and the pursuit of Happiness. That to secure these rights,

Governments are instituted among Men deriving their just powers from the consent of the governed, That whenever any Form of Government becomes destructive of these ends, it is the Right of the People to alter or to abolish it, and to institute new Government, laying its foundation on such principles, and organizing its powers in such form, as to them shall seem most likely to effect their Safety and Happiness. Prudence, indeed, will dictate that Governments long established should not be changed for light and transient causes; and accordingly all experience hath shewn, that mankind are more disposed to suffer, while evils are sufferable, than to right themselves by abolishing the forms to which they are accustomed. But when a long train of abuses and usurpations, pursuing invariably the same Object evinces a design to reduce them under absolute Despotism, it is their right, it is their duty, to throw off such Government, and to provide new Guards for their future security."

Mr. ADAMS (repeating after the Clerk) "the Right of the people to alter or to abolish it." Now Sir, if there is a principle sacred on earth and established by the instrument just read, it is the right of the people to alter, to change, to destroy the Government, if it becomes oppressive to them. There would be no such right existing, if the people had not the power, in pursuance of that right, to petition for it.

Sir, if my attachment to this Union and this Constitution could be questioned, that provision would be sufficient to refute any slanderous attacks that might be made on me. I rest that petition on the Declaration of Independence and let me tell the gentleman, and let me tell this house that they are not the only persons to whom these sentiments are familiar.

When I come to make my defense before the House, I shall show other oppressions, not only actual, but intended. I shall show that the portion of the country from which the gentleman comes are endeavoring to destroy the right of habeas corpus, the right of trial by jury, and all the rights of which the liberty of this country exists . . . and that there is a continued system and purpose to destroy all the principle of civil liberty in the free States, not for the purpose of preserving their institutions within their own limits, but to force their detested principles of slavery into all the free States. I will show that measures are systematically pursued or projected to force this country into a war. This is the state of things that exists and it is provided for in the Declaration of Independence; and if there is no other remedy for it, it is the right and duty of the people of that portion of the Union to take that remedy.

8.

"I NEED NOT SAY WHAT MATCH I WOULD TOUCH, WHAT SYSTEM ENDEAVOR TO BLOW UP"

JOHN QUINCY ADAMS was not the only American to say yes to the right of revolution. In the 1850's, thousands of white liberals and abolitionists not only proclaimed it as the "higher law," or as the "highest law of the land," but acted it out. When fugitives from the South were threatened with legal rendition to their previous condition of squalor and servitude, they had no hesitation in breaking the law to rescue them.

They rescued them by guile, threat, and violence, but mostly by violence. Riot was proven to be the best method. In Boston, in 1850, when legal racism was nationalized by the Fugitive Slave Act, plans were made to riot against the property of the slave owner. They "looted" his slave and made him a man. They organized a Vigilance Committee. It was a conspiracy against the law and order of the community.

According to its account book, still preserved, some of the most distinguished Americans of the time were fellow conspirators. Emerson; Wendell Phillips; Charles Francis Adams, the son of a President and the grandson of another; John Albion Andrews, the war governor of Massachusetts;

Dr. Samuel Gridley Howe, the humanitarian, rescuer of the blind and the mentally lost; Lysander Spooner, the Philosopher; the historians Richard Hildreth, Benjamin Mussey, and William C. Nell; the poets Lowell and Whittier, and a Channing were participants. On just three pages of accounts there stand the names of forty-seven Massachusetts preachers, of all faiths but the Roman Catholic.

Its credo was: That the law was unconstitutional and an affront to every one of the rights that are inalienable to American citizens, and therefore should be resisted. That Boston would be made a most uncomfortable place for any man low enough to enforce it. That the blacks of Boston threatened by it should not panic and leave, but know that they would be protected at all costs. That a committee of safety and vigilance would be appointed from every ward in the city to secure the rights of *any* black man from invasion by persons acting under this law. The working group became eighty men, then grew to two hundred and fifty. A good percentage of them were black. Over a dozen members of the Boston bar used their legal training to resist, defy, baffle, and nullify this law.

The hard core of the Committee was an executive of eight men: two of them were black. The chairman was Theodore Parker, a brilliant theologian engaged in what was then religion's last best hope: creating out of the best-furnished mind, religiously speaking, in America, a new form of religion, one that could explain the material world to man, its transiently baffling contradictions, its great leaps forward, so as to exult the human spirit to transcend the accidents of his material existence without fear of chaos and the dark.

For Parker, religion could be

> a very simple thing . . . very simple absolute morality, absolutely pure religion, the love of man, the love of God

acting without let or hindrance. The only form it demands is a divine life, doing the best things in the best way from the highest motives. It does not demand that all men think alike, but uprightly. . . . The relations between man and man and the duties that grow out of that relation are always the same and can never change till man ceases to be man and creation vanishes into nothing.

Parker thought he could transform man with this dint of writing and reading. He was seized of it as any creator can be seized of an idea so cosmic, so grandiose. But he put by, in all its resounding grandeur, his Paradise Regained and took on the dreariness of physical drudgery and the incessant repetition of the higher commonplaces that the role of an organizer demands. It was more than a matter of laying his work to one side. He had to become a raucous writer of leaflets and incitements. This meant his virtual expulsion from the community of scholars, to be counted now as a member of the lunatic fringe, "irresponsible and nonobjective." In that time of enormously learned men, he was considered by many the most learned of his time. But the excitement, verging on fanaticism with which Parker had to energize his life affected his balance as a scholar in the eyes of his fellows and, perhaps, destroyed it.

His stock plunged downward as an ethical leader. Responsible men then, as now, believed that if a man disobeyed one law he would be led, and would lead others, into disobeying all laws. There cannot be, they are still saying, liberty without law, and once you let the law slide there is only anarchy left. Parker disagreed. He felt that you cannot trust a people who keep a law simply because it is a law, nor should you distrust a people who will only keep a law if it is just. Laws *kept* in a racist or discriminatory way will overturn the power of human law and liberty far more than any disobedience to them.

His peers told him that he had no alternative: that if he did not decently keep the law, the nation would go down to dissolution. His answer was:

> For my own part, I would rather see my own house burnt to the ground, and my family thrown, one by one, amid the blazing rafters of my own roof, and I myself thrown in last of all, rather than have a single fugitive sent back. I would rather see this union dissolved 'till there was not a territory so large as the county of Suffolk.

When these men assisted a "fugitive," they knew that there was more than one reason why a man should flee north. It wasn't always for pure liberty: There were thieves and killers among them; if you can call anyone taking the accumulations of slavery a thief, or anyone killing a slaveholder a "killer." Most of the people in the country considered an escaped slave as much a criminal as any window smasher, rioter, or sniper in the ghettos of today. This made no difference to Parker and the rest.

Almost from the beginning, Parker and the Committee learned a sad lesson about the people of Boston; not the people really, but the men of property and standing, the responsible ones. They *were* low enough to enforce the Fugitive Law. The problem became far more complicated than merely sending invisible fugitives on their secret way. They were confronted with the case of William and Ellen Crafts, fugitive slaves, who had freely walked Boston streets until they discovered one morning that they were being stalked by police hired by their former masters. He, the master, had the full cooperation of the Federal Government, which seemed undeterred by the promise the Vigilance Committee had given that they would "secure" the safety of all fugitives.

Furthermore, they were parishioners of Parker's, and he was thus forced to make good his promises, his boasts, and he threw himself into the struggle with an ardor approaching fanaticism. He wrote broadsides which were put on the street, describing the two Southerners who had come to take back the Crafts in such a brutal and disparaging way that it was an open invitation for them to be stoned as they walked along the Boston streets. An officer of the court was bribed to inform Parker when police warrants were signed; other rewards were paid out to disloyal members of the Force for timely information on official movements. Roving bodies of men were organized to follow the slave hunters from Macon, Georgia, whenever they appeared in public, to dog them and harass them with jostlings and threats. Meetings of the Vigilance Committee were held daily, and the policy decided on was to induce the slave hunters to leave town by an accumulation of threats just short of murder. Acting within the Committee were many Negroes, hard to restrain.

William and Ellen Craft were hidden away, spending the greater part of the time at Parker's house in Exeter Place. The revolutionary pressures grew so great that Parker found some of the major premises of his religious life being transformed. With the actual hunted man under his roof he could not help but put himself in his place and one day gave him this pastoral advice:

If a man attacks you to return you to slavery, you have the right, the natural right, to resist the man unto death; but you can refuse to exercise that right if you have scruples against killing and be reduced to slavery rather than kill or even hurt the slave hunter. But Ellen is dependent on you for her protection, a duty which I feel you cannot decline, even though you must kill to carry it out and dig your own grave and the grave of a thousand men.

Parker's plan of mobbing the slave hunters every time they appeared had worked so well that the gentlemen spent most of their time in their room at the United States Hotel. Members of the Vigilance Committee invaded the hotel and began to fill the corridors and hang about, to the great fear and annoyance of the landlord . . . picketing, I suppose you would call it today. Finally the landlord's patience and composure broke down. He came to Parker and said the slave hunters wanted to see him.

Here Parker made his key play. He told them that he had come to save them from harm; that he was the only man in Boston who could save them from mob violence, that he had already diverted such an attack. They held out for a while, boasting that they could get plenty of help if they needed it, but Parker assured them that it would be suicidal for them to stay another night in Boston and that the men in the corridors were hanging about on his orders, to give the slave hunters a safe conduct to the New York train.

After an hour or so of meditation, the slave hunters left, never to return. Arrangements were then made for the Crafts to go to England. Parker married them, putting into William's right hand a Bible, and into his left, a sword, telling him that although he hated violence and held human life sacred, there were times when it was justifiable to take it — this was the same advice he would have given white men under these circumstances — but to do it, to strike down his oppressors, not from hatred, but for liberty . . . and then his action would be without sin.

Parker himself thought he would resist without weapons, fight the slaveholders with his bare hands, a common delusion among amateur revolutionaries. A few months later another slave was taken and brought to the Boston Courthouse to be remanded to his masters. Parker swung into action, getting out placards to mark the kidnapers with infamy as they passed along the streets, bribing court officers for inside information, and putting the resistance movement into motion all along the front.

This slave had the odd and lucky name of Shadrach and after he had been taken before the Commissioner a man with the power to send him back without a formal trial, upon the simple identification of his master, or his agent, he was put into a room under the custodianship of one Pat Riley, a deputy marshal.

Lewis Hayden, a popular and extremely resourceful Negro, a fugitive himself, organized a group of Negroes, teamsters and mechanics, well-known around the Courthouse, and laughing and fooling and acting in their expected role of amiable incompetency, they stumbled by the careless guards at the Courthouse door, made their way to the room in which Shadrach was confined, and burst into it, reducing Pat Riley to shocked impotence. Lewis Hayden snatched up Riley's sword of office and threatened him into continued nonresistance while Shadrach left his fiery furnace, surrounded by his friends. The other court officers were of that class of white racists to whom all men of color look alike and so Shadrach escaped. Lewis Hayden and several other blacks were later arrested and tried . . . but acquitted because it so happened that the foreman of the jury was a member of the Vigilance Committee and, in fact, the very man who had driven Shadrach in his carriage to make the train connections for the fugitive's flight into Canada.

But with each case, the opposition got tougher, the lapses and fissures in the apparatus of oppression were tightened up, forcing the passive liberals and the purely cerebral or ethical advocates of fair play, to the sidelines. There was much talk in Washington that the Shadrach rescue was treasonable; Daniel Webster said it was. Threats were made to send whole regiments of regular U.S. troops to Boston to enforce the law. On April 8, 1851, the third attempt to placate the angry South and "save the Union" was made, with the capture by guile of a slave named Sims. He was secretly taken, secretly confined, and when the news came out, the Courthouse was surrounded not only with a cordon of armed men, but with chains, so that the august Justices of the Massachusetts Supreme Judicial Court had to stoop under them, in symbolic obeisance, to get to their mighty and impartial seats.

The Vigilance Committee tried every legal and illegal trick they could think of; then desperately, one morning at three A.M. they made their way to the Courthouse with arms full of mattresses with the thought that somehow they might get Sims to jump from his room onto them and be saved. It was growing very difficult now for Parker to raise forces for open resistance. Most of the militant black men were either in jail or scattered by the prosecutions of the Shadrach rescuers. The Garrisonian abolitionists were also nonresistants and would not raise a hand in violence against anyone.

At a tense meeting presided over by Horace Mann, two desperate schemes were discussed, the jump idea and a notion that perhaps they could charter a ship and intercept the brig that was to take Sims back to slavery. The latter plan was laid aside as impracticable, not because it was piracy, but because it was not certain that Sims would be sent back on a ship. But when the Vigilantes arrived at Courthouse Square that morning, they found assembled a hundred policemen and a hundred local volunteers in behalf of slavery, armed with straight, double-edged Roman swords . . . the same sort, ironically enough, that John Brown used for his Pottawatamie executions of five proslavery partisans. Looking up, they saw workmen fitting iron bars over the window of the room in which Sims was confined, and they realized that all conspiracies get to be two-edged, and that there was now an agent of the authorities inside the Vigilance Committee. Sims was sent back that morning, and there was a later rumor that he had been whipped to death upon his arrival in Georgia . . . but this was not true, only whipped carefully, and repeatedly, nearly to death.

Parker himself was not allowed to go unwhipped for this, and his other titanic struggles to serve the state with his conscience. The leading newspaper in Boston, the *Advertiser*, ran this in the place reserved for its most urgent and direct appeals and incitements to community opinion:

> Self-proclaimed Teachers of Piety like Theodore Parker may agitate too frequently and too far and in an evil hour, find themselves implicated in an act of high treason. The overt act may be committed at a time they know not of, quite unexpectedly to them. They may be engaged, perhaps, in writing libels against the judiciary, or in composing pious tracts upon the expediency of perjury. They may be remote from the action, but however remote, their participation in the conspiracy will be shown. It will be shown that they conspired for the object, were active in promoting it, were members of a vigilance committee, had talked and written, preached and prayed in its behalf, and agitated as freely as they had a mind to. Thus the connection will be established, and the law, as laid down by the Supreme Judicial Court of the United States, will proclaim them traitors and the halter will prevent them from teaching anymore piety.

Despite this threat of indictment for treason Parker and the other members of the Vigilance Committee had no hesitation about going into action again in May, 1854, when they heard that another fugitive, Anthony Burns, had been arrested in Boston and was about to be remanded to his claimant in Virginia. They, first of all, supplied the best legal counsel available, Richard Henry Dana, to fight the question out in the courts, but before the decision was even given, they made plans to rescue Burns by force and violence.

At a mass meeting in Faneuil Hall, on the night of May 26, after a series of inflammatory speeches and resolutions . . . one being: "That which is not just is not the law, and that which is not the law should not be obeyed" . . . the crowd left to storm the Boston Courthouse, where Burns was confined, and rescue him by brute force. This was in effect a direct attack upon the Federal Government, which was using

the return of Burns to his so-called master as a pledge to the
South that their peculiar institution would be respected and
enforced to the letter of the law. The seemingly spontaneous
eruption of the people at the meeting had been planned
ahead. There were already men — led by Thomas Wentworth
Higginson, later a Colonel in a Black Regiment, and a Martin Stowell, head of the Worcester Temperance Society, who
carried a very intemperate pistol in his belt — at the Courthouse armed with axes and a battering ram to break down the
doors as the crowd came up.

The timing of the onslaught was confused and bad. It
was more a riot than the intended conspiracy. When the inflamed crowd arrived from the meeting they began to throw
rocks at the Courthouse. Every window on the south side was
broken. The judges of the Superior Court, waiting that night
for a hung jury to make up its mind, had all the windows
smashed in their retiring room. The door of the Courthouse
was smashed in, and the rioters attempted to enter, led by
Higginson. He was immediately attacked by the police inside
with clubs and sabers and driven against the wall. His friend,
Martin Stowell, ran to the opening and fired point-blank at
the police. One fell, mortally wounded. Higginson wrested
himself free and ran out into the mob.

During this time shots were being fired by the rioters at
the building and being returned from inside. At one point
there was a standoff and a silence; the broken door stood
shattered and agape. Amos Bronson Alcott, armed only with
a cane, ascended the Courthouse steps in his stately way, stood
a moment at the yawning entrance, and said to the rioters,
"Why are we not within?" Someone shot at him from the
inside, nobody followed him from the outside, so he turned
around and walked unhurriedly back into the crowd.

Shortly after this, the Boston Artillery Company, taking
their usual Friday night drill on the streets of the town, came
marching into the Courthouse Square. The rioters, mistaking
them for the U.S. Marines, coming to restore order, quieted

down, and the Boston Police quickly arrested nine obvious offenders, and dragged them off to the city jail.

One was a Harvard student named Albert G. Browne, Jr., whose father was a member of the Governor's Council. Martin Stowell was arrested, still carrying a pistol with one shot missing. Four of the men arrested were black and armed. Lewis Hayden, the black revolutionary who had been next to Higginson entering the Courthouse at the height of the scuffle, had drawn and fired directly at Watson Freeman, the U.S. Marshal. It passed under his raised arm. When Parker heard this he said, "Why did he not hit him?"

Higginson and Hayden were not arrested. Higginson made his way back to Worcester, where he occupied the pulpit of a church, between barrels of fresh fish on a butcher's cart. The nine prisoners were charged in the police court with felonious assault; that they collectively, with firearms loaded with powder and ball, did kill and murder the deputy Bachelder. They were held over for murder. A reporter named Drew from Worcester got to Martin Stowell in prison and was able to smuggle out the incriminating pistol.

The press made Parker the leading rioter.

> Let us see where rests the responsibility, before God and man, for this murder. It was not the person who, in a moment of intense excitement, inflicted the fatal wound upon the person of James Bachelder, who is responsible for this deed; *but it is the men who artfully inflamed his passions, and then left him to their uncontrolled exercise. . . .* It is they alone who are GUILTY OF MURDER . . . but if anyone is more guilty than another, it is the Reverend Theodore Parker, for it was he who put the motion to adjourn to Court Square. . . .

Attempts were then made to have a Federal Grand Jury then sitting find a true bill against Parker and other prominent members of the Committee for murder, or treason, but they failed.

Dr. Charles Jackson, Emerson's brother-in-law was the

medical examiner, and he declared, perhaps out of revolutionary duplicity, that Bachelder had been stabbed, not shot, and it became very difficult to tie the nine men any further to the murder clause. Three other well-known radicals were arrested; one a black man named Nelson Hopewell, who was found to be carrying a Malay kris, which could have been the murder weapon. But the county District Attorney was a secret sympathizer of the movement, and the murder charges were dropped on all the men, although they were still held for rioting. Henry Thoreau, some weeks later, during a speech given at Framingham under the auspices of the Massachusetts Antislavery Society, made an impassioned plea to his audience to get these rioters out of prison. . . .

> I had thought the house was on fire and not the prairie but though several of the citizens of Massachusetts are now in prison for attempting to rescue a slave from her own clutches, not one of the speakers at the meeting expressed regret for it, not one even referred to it . . . [Fame] praises till she is hoarse the easy exploit of the Boston Tea party, but will be comparatively silent about the braver and more disinterestedly heroic attack on the Boston Court House, simply because it was unsuccessful. . . . Covered with disgrace, the State has sat down coolly to try for their lives and liberties the men who attempted to do its duty for it. And this is called *justice* . . . My thoughts are murder to the State and involuntarily go plotting against her.

These men were eventually let go, but the attack on Parker and other leading members of the Committee grew very intense. A special Grand Jury was empaneled and charged with the responsibility of indicting those who resist an officer when carrying out his duty. Judge Benjamin Robbins Curtis, on the U.S. Supreme Court, which then sat on cases in the Federal Districts during their spare time, gave this charge.

> My instruction to you is, that language addressed to persons who immediately afterwards commit an offense actu-

ally intended by the speaker to incite those addressed to commit it, and adapted thus to incite them, is such a councilling, or advising to the crime as the law contemplates, and the person so inciting others is liable to be indicted as a principal.

If the nine men arrested on the night of the riot had been indicted for murder, as proposed, Parker would have been tried for murder along with them. As it was when the true bill came against him, Wendell Phillips, Stowell, Higginson, and some others, from a jury on which the brother-in-law of Judge Curtis was serving, it was merely for a misdemeanor for obstructing an officer.

The crime, as alleged, did carry the sentence of a year's imprisonment and a heavy fine. Parker wrote a very brilliant "defense" for his day in court. It pertains marvelously to the questions of today, to the police who act constantly with brutality and retaliation against black citizens. He never denied he obstructed the law at the time. He said, over and over again, "I will confess more than the government can prove."

But he claimed the U.S. Marshal, at the time the rioters obstructed him, was violating the law himself.

For if he were violating the law and thereby injuring some other man, and I obstructed him in that injury, then I am free from all legal guilt, and did a citizen's duty in obstructing his illegal conduct. Now it appears that he was kidnapping and stealing Anthony Burns for the purpose of making him a slave . . . to have acted under the Fugitive Slave Bill . . . is that bill Constitutional?

The Constitution of the United States is the people's power of attorney by which they authorize certain servants, called legislative, judicial, and executive officers, to do certain matters, and things in a certain way, but prohibit them from doing, in the name of the people, any thing except those things specified, or those in any but the way pointed out.

Parker felt that the Constitution was drawn to establish justice and domestic tranquility . . . and liberty. Arrest, imprisonment, and trial, without all the rights of due process, were unconstitutional, and had not to be obeyed . . . and should be obstructed. He felt, furthermore, that the people should make the decisions about the guilt or innocence of the men brought before them, and not the judges. They were not to take the opinion of the court because it was almost always their "purchased official opinion," which the government pays for, and so was of no value whatsoever. And if it was their *personal* opinion, everybody knew already what it was; it was time-serving, and of no possible value. It was obvious that a country could not have tranquility by oppressing its citizens and making them slaves. And if the jury felt that the Fugitive Slave Law did not promote liberty, or general welfare, then it was unconstitutional and the police were acting *against* the peace of the United States. Thus it was "the right of every citizen to obstruct their illegal wickedness."

Parker's defense was never given in court. No jury ever heard it because the judges saw a tiny "flaw in the indictment" long before they would let a Boston jury hear Parker tell them what laws they should obey and what laws they should resist. His case was dismissed on the motion of the U.S. District Attorney.

Burns was returned to Virginia at enormous expense, and only with the muscle of the Federal Government. The Adjutant General of the Army was ordered to Boston, Government troops poured in from Rhode Island and New Hampshire, and soldiers in New York City were kept under arms in a forty-eight-hour alert during the emergency. Fifteen hundred Local Militia with bayonets had to keep the crowds back during Burns's walk to the ship to carry him away. Federal troops with cannon guarded intersections. Bricks and crowbars were thrown at the procession, along with bottles filled with vitriol — the Molotov cocktails of the time. The angry crowd broke through the lines at one point and had to be sabered back by the mounted Massachusetts Lancers. No slave was ever again seized in Massachusetts. Nor was anyone actually punished for taking part in the riot.

Some may feel that it is a far cry from the "rioting" of Theodore Parker and the Boston Brahmins to the disorderly eruptions in the ghettos. Parker and his kind had no difficulty investing their acts of lawlessness with all the trappings of revolutionary virtue. They easily made them seem noble, and they were noble. Parker felt he had the hereditary right to be revolutionary.

> I drew my first breath in a little town not far off, a poor little town where the farmers and mechanics first unsheathed that revolutionary sword, which, after eight years of hewing, clove asunder the Gordian knot that bound America to the British yoke. That [Lexington Green] Monument covers the bones of my own kinsfolk: it was their blood which reddened the long green grass of Lexington. It is my own name which stands chiseled on that stone the tall captain who marshalled his fellow farmers and mechanics into stern array and spoke such brave and dangerous words as opened the war of American Independence — the last to leave the field — was my father's father. I learned to read out of his Bible, and with a musket he that day captured from the foe, I learned another religious lesson, that REBELLION TO TYRANTS IS OBEDIENCE TO GOD.

The names of the black men that have died, whose blood has reddened the green grass in every state in the Union, in acts of rebellion braver than Parker's grandfather's, are not recorded on any battle monument. The beautiful words of Parker and Jefferson are never allotted to them — although their hereditary right to revolution is infinitely more valid than ours. They know that in the South they made the milk and honey come, nursed the young cotton and corn, raised the cool white Grecian mansions, and then they were homeless. They led the shining stallions into the deep blue grass, only to have their flashing hoofbeats turn and tread them down. When they pleaded for their rights, in the name of Crispus Attucks, who fell before the fire of tyrants, they were answered by their country with curses and chains. When, for Jesus' sake they cried for mercy, they got the whip. They appeal to American humanity, and it hates them, scorns, slanders, and disowns them. The outspreading wings of American charity, boasting of its ability to give hope and shelter to the world, refuse to cover the black man and his wife and child. To them its bones are brass and its feathers are iron. Although there is never a day in this country when the black people are not scourged by poverty, cruelty, and neglect, when they do rise and go into the street to resist a society they detest, and smash that part of the society they detest most of all, people who should know better turn their backs, resent them for destroying "property," cannot hear their voices, feel no guilt themselves and dump all the guilt on the oppressed blacks.

There has never been a time in this country when the black people have not resisted the tyranny over them. But we have seen to it that their revolutionary energies become dissipated in mere violence . . . and have caused, and then decried, their inability to organize them into a form of progressive force. The story of heroic individual episodes, and in particular the ones in which they were joined by whites, have been dropped from the historical cannon, or deliberately misrepresented. All the lessons of the trial-and-error method of self-liberation have in this way been expunged, and it has become harder and harder for the black people to act out their own revolutionary identity, and almost impossible for the whites. Both of us have had to accept as our own history the spurious one of our masked oppressors, an American identity of bloody victories, genocides, conquests, and hundred-year struggles for markets and opportunities for human exploitation.

Our roots cry hungrily for the juices of another identity . . . for the merging of our consciousness with other and earlier Americans who were not exploiters, who were not racists, who were not victims. Many of us live with a fire in our deeps, in our sub-guts. It does not burn with a gemlike flame. It is more like a fire on a dump, struggling for life, and then inundated again and again with worn-out trash so that we are mostly strangled with the sour smoke of our own ineffectual burnings. Sometimes someone from the past and the present pokes enough at us to open us up and burn free . . . we flame up and consume the trash and garbage heaped on us each day. The fires have been burning hot, lately.

Side with the light, Thoreau said, over a hundred years ago, giving his testimony about the Anthony Burns case and the arrest of the men who rioted in the effort to free him. What he said then is as true today:

> The majority of men are not men of principle . . . while their brothers and sisters are being scourged and hung for loving liberty . . . it is the mismanagement of wood and iron and stone that concerns them. (They say) Do what you will, O Government, with my wife and children, my mother and brother, my father and sister, I will obey your commands to the letter. It will grieve me if you hurt them, if you deliver them to overseers to be hunted by hounds or to be whipped to death; but, nevertheless, I will peaceably pursue my chosen calling on this fair earth, until perchance, one day, when I have put on mourning for the dead, I shall have persuaded you to relent. Such is the attitude, such are the words of Massachusetts.
>
> Rather than do this, I need not say what match I would touch, what system endeavor to blow up; but as I love my life, I would side with the light, and let the dark earth roll from under me, calling my mother and brother to follow.

Siding with the light I believe that the eighty riots in the ghettos of America in the summer of 1967 were revolutionary alternatives to present degradation and future genocide. I believe also that the line of resistance the black people are taking will lead them inexorably into setting up a new underground railroad in which fugitives from white justice may be passed from city to city, state to state, and country to country. This must be done to preserve their valuable lives and resources from the destruction of the oppressor. It may force them into taking white hostages and holding them against the safe return of their own.

If I deny black people this, or any other form of resistance for which white men have been applauded and venerated, I am not only a coward, but a racist. To me they are citizens and men in the revolutionary sense. They cannot be denied telling us the truths that only upheavals and outbreaks can tell . . . the terrible judgments which prove without any doubt that the fate of black and white in this country is indivisible forever.

Therefore I must join them, defend them, explain them . . . recruit for them. Their history alone has become our only redemption, the only road to American fulfillment, to manhood, and womanhood. The only road to a life of principle and ideals, to the answers to the great and accursed questions of personal independence, the citizen's relation to the state, the inalienable right of resistance, the wrongs of war, poverty, racism, and every other form of human denial.

I do not wish, any longer, to be guilty concerning my brother.

Pol Sci